Discrimination in Society

Sex Discrimination

Peggy J. Parks

ReferencePoint Press

San Diego, CA

About the Author
Peggy J. Parks is an author who has written dozens of educational books on a wide variety of topics for teens and young adults. She lives in Muskegon, Michigan, a town she says inspires her writing because of its location on the shores of beautiful Lake Michigan.

For more information, contact:
ReferencePoint Press, Inc.
PO Box 27779
San Diego, CA 92198
www.ReferencePointPress.com

LIBRARY OF CONGRESS CATALOGING-IN-PUBLICATION DATA

Name: Parks, Peggy J., 1951– author.
Title: Sex Discrimination/by Peggy J. Parks.
Description: San Diego, CA: ReferencePoint Press, [2019] | Series:
  Discrimination in Society | Audience: Grade 9 to 12. | Includes
  bibliographical references and index.
Identifiers: LCCN 2018018329 (print) | LCCN 2018021156 (ebook) | ISBN
  9781682823903 (eBook) | ISBN 9781682823897 (hardback)
Subjects: LCSH: Sex discrimination in employment—Juvenile literature. |
  Sexual harassment—Juvenile literature. | Sex discrimination against
  men—Law and legislation—Juvenile literature.
Classification: LCC HD6060 (ebook) | LCC HD6060 .P37 2019 (print) | DDC
  331.4/1330973—dc23
LC record available at https://lccn.loc.gov/2018018329

CONTENTS

A Matter of Fairness and Respect

AJ Vandermeyden had a good job as a sales representative, but she dreamed of working at Tesla. She had long been impressed with the high-tech electric vehicle and solar energy company, and she admired its ambitious cofounder, Elon Musk. So in April 2013, when Vandermeyden was offered a job at Tesla, she accepted the position. She would be working as a product specialist at its corporate headquarters in Palo Alto, California.

Vandermeyden thrived in her new job and worked hard to prove herself. Her performance impressed management, and within a year she was promoted to an engineering position. The promotion involved switching to Tesla's automotive manufacturing plant in Fremont, California, where vehicles are assembled by robotic equipment. Vandermeyden was thrilled at the chance to work in this futuristic environment— but she soon encountered something that was shocking as well as troubling. Her new job exposed her to an environment that was rife with sex discrimination.

Fighting Back

Vandermeyden worked with a group of eight employees, all of whom were men. Soon after starting her new position, she was dismayed to learn that she earned less than all of her male coworkers, even though she was equally or more qualified. After she found a critical error in machinery and pointed it out to management, Vandermeyden's male coworkers were given credit for the discovery. Other aspects of the job were troubling as well, such as an area of the plant that female workers referred to as the "predator zone." Male workers whistled and called out sexist, offensive remarks whenever women walked through the area. "They all started hooting and hollering and whistling,"[1] says Vandermeyden. Finally, she decided to consult an attorney, and in September 2016 she filed a lawsuit against Tesla. This action, Vandermeyden hoped, would spur Tesla management into making needed changes to stop sex discrimination.

In what seemed like a positive response, Tesla held a meeting in which female employees were encouraged to talk about their personal experiences. Many said that they, too, had been subjected to ongoing sex discrimination and harassment by their male coworkers. Afterward, Vandermeyden believed that her complaints and those of other female employees would be addressed—but that did not happen. In May 2017 she was asked to meet with Tesla's chief people officer, who gave her an ultimatum: to resign and be assisted in finding a new job or be terminated immediately. Vandermeyden was stunned. Despite all that had happened, she was still devoted to Tesla and wanted to keep working for the company. When she refused to resign, however, she was promptly fired. Vandermeyden and her attorney claimed it was an act of retaliation, but Tesla management disagreed, saying there were other reasons for her firing.

Unjust and Unfair

When people are treated unfairly because of their gender, it is considered sex discrimination (or gender discrimination), which is illegal under federal law. As defined by the US Equal Employment Opportunity Commission (EEOC), the federal agency that enforces discrimination laws, sex discrimination specifically pertains to place of employment. Being tied to someone's job is what differentiates sex discrimination from the closely related term, *sexism*. Sexism

Sexual harassment affects both males and females, but it is females who most often experience persistently hostile or offensive work environments. Those who are subjected to this type of behavior often feel depressed and anxious—and many are forced to quit their jobs.

also involves beliefs and biases about gender, but it is not necessarily tied to employment.

Sexual harassment, which is also illegal, is considered a type of sex discrimination. Referred to as "sex discrimination harassment" by the EEOC, this type of discrimination may involve unwelcome sexual advances, inappropriate touching, requests for sexual favors, or other verbal or physical harassment of a sexual nature. It does not include occasional teasing or joking, even if that is considered offensive to some people. In order for behavior to be considered sexual harassment, it must be persistent and create a hostile or offensive work environment. It affects both males and females, although females are sexually harassed most often. In a December 2017 survey by the Pew Research Center, 20 percent of women and 7 percent of men reported experiencing sexual harassment at work.

Whatever form it takes, sex discrimination causes distress for those who experience it. They lose enthusiasm for their jobs and may dread going to work. Depression and/or anxiety are common effects, as is a loss of confidence and harm to one's overall well-being. People often find it difficult to know who they can trust within their workplace. Brandon Charles observed this lack of trust when he started working at Social Finance in Southern California. Charles was responsible for managing a team of five people. He knew something was wrong the first time he asked the team to be candid and let him know if there were problems within the company that he could help address. "When I said that, the way they reacted—it was almost like they were victims of war," says Charles. "They literally looked at me, and one said, 'Why should we trust you?'"[2]

Troubling Prevalence

In the past, people rarely discussed sex discrimination, and it was not granted much publicity. That has changed in recent years, largely because of numerous high-profile individuals being called out for discriminatory and harassing behavior. Some of the most well known of these individuals are film producer Harvey Weinstein, comedians Bill Cosby and Louis C.K., actor Kevin Spacey, Senator Al Franken, television host Ryan Seacrest, and *Today Show* anchor Matt Lauer.

> "People would be appalled at some of the behaviour that goes on at the workplace."[3]
>
> —Therese Lawless, an employment attorney who specializes in sex discrimination cases

Research has shown that sex discrimination is widespread throughout the United States. "It's far worse than people know," says Therese Lawless, a prominent employment attorney who specializes in sex discrimination cases. "People would be appalled at some of the behaviour that goes on at the workplace."[3] The December 2017 Pew Research Center survey found that

42 percent of employed women and 22 percent of employed men have experienced some type of sex discrimination. According to a January 2018 report by the EEOC, the agency received 25,606 sex discrimination complaints and 6,696 sexual harassment complaints during 2017.

Although people in all sorts of jobs and workplaces have been affected by sex discrimination, it is known for being especially prevalent in science, technology, engineering, and mathematics (STEM) careers. Females in STEM jobs are affected by sexual harassment far more than males. According to a January 2018 Pew Research Center survey, 50 percent of women in STEM jobs have experienced sex discrimination at work, compared with 19 percent of men.

> "It's shocking in this day and age that this is still a fight we have to have."[4]
>
> —AJ Vandermeyden, a former Tesla employee who sued the company for sex discrimination

Changes Sorely Needed

Sex discrimination is not a new problem, but awareness of its prevalence has soared in recent years. More and more people are speaking out against it, despite knowing that there are risks involved—such as losing one's job. Speaking of her own experience and that of other women, Vandermeyden says, "It's shocking in this day and age that this is still a fight we have to have."[4] Still, she and others who have taken a stand against sex discrimination—and paid the price for it—hope that what they have done eventually pays off in sex discrimination being reduced or eliminated altogether.

Sex Discrimination in the Workplace

Throughout the United States, in virtually every type of industry and workplace, sex discrimination is a common problem. It affects males as well as females, but research has shown that females are discriminated against far more often than their male counterparts. Sex discrimination is known to occur at every level of the employment process, starting with the review of job applicant credentials. Consequently, even getting in the door is often more difficult for female job seekers than males. Researchers Caryl Rivers and Rosalind C. Barnett, who specialize in sex discrimination and related workplace issues, write, "Her resume may look just like his, but because the name is Jane and not Joe, recruiters may not give a second look."[5]

Blatant Bias

One groundbreaking study that exposed this discriminatory preference for male applicants was conducted by social scientist Corinne A. Moss-Racusin and her colleagues in 2012. Moss-Racusin has devoted her career to understanding how gender bias (the often unconscious preference for one gender over another) can lead to sex discrimination in the workplace. For the study, the researchers created a fictitious résumé of a college student applying for a science laboratory manager position. They made two versions of the exact same résumé: one for a male applicant named John and the other for a female applicant named Jennifer. More than one hundred professors of science (biology, chemistry, and/or physics) from universities throughout the United States agreed to review a résumé. Each was randomly assigned one from "John" or one from "Jennifer."

After the reviews were complete, the professors had overwhelmingly rated the male applicant as more competent and qualified for the job than the female applicant. This rating, and thus the respondents' preference for the ideal candidate, was clearly based on gender bias. The study authors explain, "Because all other information was held constant between conditions, any differences in participants' responses are attributable to the gender of the student." Interestingly, the professors' own gender had no effect on their bias toward a particular candidate. "Our results revealed that both male and female faculty judged a female student to be less competent and less worthy of being hired than an identical male student,"[6] the study authors write. In addition to discriminatory hiring, the professors were also willing to offer the male applicant a higher annual salary than the female candidate, as well as more opportunities for career mentoring.

When the study was published, it generated a buzz among researchers and university faculty members. Although many were receptive of the findings, others questioned the study's validity, with some denouncing it as junk science. In an effort to understand why the study evoked such negative reactions, researchers from Montana State University conducted their own review in 2015. They recruited several hundred participants, many of whom worked in STEM careers, whose assignment was to read the 2012 study and rank how favorably (or unfavorably) they viewed the findings. In general, male reviewers ranked the study less favorably than female reviewers. This response was most pronounced among participants working in STEM careers, with males ranking the study as significantly less important and less well written than did females in STEM careers.

As for why males and females viewed the study so differently, researchers are not certain. It likely has some connection with people's own beliefs and biases about gender that influence how

Many Working Women Have Experienced Sex Discrimination

Forty-two percent of working women say they have experienced some type of sex discrimination at work, according to a 2017 Pew Research Center survey. When asked about specific types of discrimination, the two types cited most were earning less than a man doing the same job and being treated as if they were not competent. The survey also found that women were about twice as likely as men to say they have experienced sex discrimination at work.

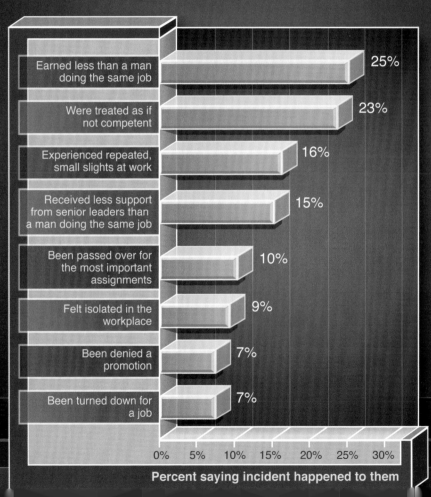

Which, if any, of the following has happened to you?

Earned less than a man doing the same job	25%
Were treated as if not competent	23%
Experienced repeated, small slights at work	16%
Received less support from senior leaders than a man doing the same job	15%
Been passed over for the most important assignments	10%
Felt isolated in the workplace	9%
Been denied a promotion	7%
Been turned down for a job	7%

0%   5%   10%   15%   20%   25%   30%

Percent saying incident happened to them

they see the world—many of which stem from sexist attitudes that have existed in society for generations. Because of those personal beliefs and biases, people often feel most receptive toward what they already believe to be true. Thus, since women in STEM careers are exposed to sex discrimination, they know firsthand that it exists and would tend to believe research that reinforces that. In contrast, men are not affected by sex discrimination as often as women, so they might react negatively toward research that contradicts their beliefs. Ian Handley, one of the Montana State University researchers, explains, "Men, they don't see it every day and don't think it's a problem."[7]

Two Sets of Standards

When women are asked about their personal experiences in the workplace, many say they are held to different standards than their male colleagues. Indeed, research has shown that certain behaviors, including aggressiveness and even rudeness, are more tolerated when exhibited by males than by females. Actress Jennifer Lawrence has experienced this often in her line of work. She recalls one occasion when she spoke her opinion clearly and bluntly but was not at all aggressive. She says the man she was working with looked at her and said, "Whoa! We're all on the same team here!" as though Lawrence had exploded in anger, which she had not. "I was so shocked because nothing that I said was personal, offensive, or to be honest, wrong," she says. "All I hear and see all day are men speaking their opinions, and I give mine in the same exact manner, and you would have thought I had said something offensive."[8]

> "All I hear and see all day are men speaking their opinions, and I give mine in the same exact manner, and you would have thought I had said something offensive."[8]
>
> —Jennifer Lawrence, an Academy Award–winning actress

Surveys have indicated that the more competent women are in their jobs, the more harshly they tend to be judged by their peers.

The Dual Disadvantage for Women of Color

Women's experiences with workplace sex discrimination are well documented and range from fewer opportunities for advancement to being paid lower salaries than their male counterparts. Women of color face even greater challenges, according to a 2017 study by LeanIn.org and McKinsey & Company. The study determined that women of color, especially black women, face more obstacles throughout their careers. In contrast to white women, they receive less support from management, face a steeper path to leadership, and rarely (if ever) are able to interact with senior leaders. For instance, 40 percent of white women agreed that managers defend them and/or their work, compared with 28 percent of black women. Similarly, 59 percent of white women said they have equal opportunity for growth in their workplace, compared with 48 percent of black women.

Erica Joy Baker, who is African American, worked in engineering at Google from 2006 to 2016. She says that the vast majority of opportunities went to employees who fit a particular mold: white and male. "Throughout my career at Google," says Baker, "there was the standard thing: 'I know you want to work on this thing, but we're going to let a white dude work on it. Sorry, we're going to let a white dude go ahead of you.' That was really frustrating."

Quoted in Sheelah Kolhatkar, "The Tech Industry's Discrimination Problem," *New Yorker*, November 20, 2017. www.newyorker.com.

For instance, if women are confident, strong, self-assured, and unafraid to speak their minds, they are often perceived as unpleasant. Men who exhibit those same characteristics are judged very differently. They are viewed as motivated, self-assured, and go-getters who are driven to succeed. "Women who display competence often pay a price," say Rivers and Barnett. "They are seen by both men and women as unlikable—unfeminine, aggressive, conniving and untrustworthy."[9] People have their own reasons for forming such biased conclusions. Researchers theorize that it is related to societal norms: the old-fashioned expectation that women should be feminine, soft spoken, and gentle rather than displaying boldness and other qualities that are characteristically viewed as masculine.

Discriminatory Work Environment

A 2017 survey called *Women in the Workplace* revealed that women often experience a workplace that is "skewed in favor of men."[10] More than seventy thousand employees from eighty-two different companies shared their opinions during the survey, and several major trends were identified. One is that women are typically promoted less often than men from the very early stages of their careers. Entry-level females, for example, are 18 percent less likely to be promoted than their male peers. This can have a ripple effect on a company's overall management composition, resulting in a far greater number of males in top management than females.

Another trend identified in the survey was that women of color, especially black women, face even more workplace obstacles due to discrimination than their white female counterparts. And like other studies before it, the survey revealed that males and females view the issue of sex discrimination differently. Men, for instance, are more likely to believe that the workplace is equitable, whereas females disagree because their personal experience has proved otherwise.

Sex Discrimination in the Military

Such discriminatory experiences have been reported by women in all types of employment, including the US military. As of April 2017, women make up about 15 percent of the 1.34 million active-duty military personnel and serve in all branches, including the army, air force, navy, and marines. In each of these branches, sex discrimination has been documented. According to US Army captain Elizabeth M. Trobaugh, military women are subject to continuous stereotyping, such as whether they are capable of performing their duties as well as men or even whether they belong in the military at all. "These attitudes and beliefs threaten the integrity of the Armed Forces as well as their mission,"[11] says Trobaugh.

Men in the military have also spoken out about the high prevalence of discrimination against women. Roger Misso, a lieutenant with the US Navy, has observed rampant sex discrimination, starting when he was a new officer just out of flight training. Misso refers to a "toxic culture of gender discrimination and inequality" in the military. He recalls a female officer in his squadron who was treated deplorably by male officers because they resented her being there. "They kept tallies of how often they made her cry," says Misso. "[They] talked about her behind her back like she was unintelligent or promiscuous, and undermined her at every opportunity with senior leaders around the ship. It was nasty, and it was constant." According to Misso, military women are discriminated against not because they lack skills or the ability to do their jobs but simply because they are female. "In any workplace," says Misso, "discrimination of nearly one-fifth of the workforce would be shocking. In the military, it is indefensible."[12]

One of the problems most often cited by female military personnel is how seldom they are promoted to higher ranks compared with their male counterparts. Women who do get promoted are often accused of being advanced solely because of their gender,

US Marines salute during a ceremony. In some areas of the military, women are subjected to rampant sex discrimination. Some female service members experience bias in everyday interactions and in promotions.

rather than earning the promotion fairly. Bridget E. Lyons, an attorney with the US Air Force, was repeatedly passed over for promotions. "I went up for promotion multiple times, five or six times in a two-year time period, and got passed over every time for men," she says. "No woman had been promoted in that division in that office. Ever."[13] Lyons also experienced a hostile work environment, which she attributes to her speaking out about not getting promoted.

Lyons sued the air force for sex discrimination. Her lawsuit dragged on for several years, and in February 2017 she was awarded a $140,000 settlement. Air force officials emphasized

Sexism Causes Harm

Many people are familiar with the most serious, blatant kinds of sex discrimination, such as qualified job applicants being disregarded solely based on gender or women being paid lower salaries than men for performing the same work. But the nature and impact of more subtle sexist actions are not as well understood, nor are they always taken seriously. One example is a manager asking a female employee who has just returned to work after maternity leave if she is sure she can balance motherhood with her job responsibilities. A woman might be told that females are not well suited for traditionally male occupations, or she might have her opinions be ignored while attending an all-male meeting. These subtle acts of sexism, according to Australian researcher Victor Sojo, are often not taken seriously because they may seem harmless when compared to more overt acts of sex discrimination. But his research has shown that reasoning to be false.

Sojo conducted a study that involved comparing different levels of sex discrimination, from seemingly mild and subtle to the most blatant, and found that all forms are equally harmful to the well-being of women. The effects include mental and physical health problems, dissatisfaction with their jobs and relationships with colleagues, and overall lower life satisfaction. "Far from being a second tier issue," says Sojo, "all the forms of sexism evaluated were as detrimental to women's occupational well-being as other job stressors that are often considered major problems at work."

Victor Sojo, "Overt or Covert, Sexism at Work Causes Real Harm," Conversation, October 9, 2014. https://theconversation.com.

that the settlement was not an admission of any wrongdoing, but Lyons felt vindicated and relieved. Still, she warns that her case is but one sign of a much larger and more pervasive problem in the US military, as well as in society in general. "It's not just some pie-in-the-sky thing," says Lyons. "It happens to your very neighbor. It happens to the woman down the street or the woman you see in the grocery store."[14]

> "I went up for promotion multiple times, five or six times in a two-year time period, and got passed over every time for men. . . . No woman had been promoted in that division in that office. Ever."[13]
>
> —Bridget E. Lyons, an attorney with the US Air Force

High-Tech Discrimination

The male-dominated tech industry is known for being as discriminatory toward females as the US military. Many well-known tech companies have been cited, and sometimes sued, for sex discrimination, including Microsoft, Twitter, Facebook, Oracle, Uber, and Google. For an April 2017 *Atlantic* article, journalist Liza Mundy interviewed dozens of women who work in the tech industry. During the interviews, the women expressed their love for many aspects of working in tech. "They love the problem-solving, the camaraderie, the opportunity for swift advancement and high salaries, the fun of working with the technology itself," says Mundy. Despite all that they love about their careers, however, every one of the women has faced sex discrimination at work. Mundy explains, "All of them had stories about incidents that, no matter how quick or glancing, chipped away at their sense of belonging and expertise."[15]

One of these women is Tracy Chou, who experienced sex discrimination from the very start of her career in the tech industry. After earning a master's degree from Stanford University, Chou became a software engineer. During one of her first jobs at a high-tech start-up, she was shocked by the sexist environment and inappropriate remarks about women. "I loved coding," she says. "But I just felt something was off. I felt out of place, and I had serious questions about whether I was going to stay in tech."[16] At one point Chou found a critical flaw in the company's software code and reported it. Her engineering team, on which she was the only female, dismissed her concern, but she persisted. Finally, a male coworker saw that she was right and backed her up. Only then was Chou's concern taken seriously, and she was still not treated equally or as a person with competence or expertise.

In 2016 a group of seven senior-level women from the tech industry conducted a survey called *Elephant in the Valley*. The survey involved more than two hundred women with at least ten years of experience working in Silicon Valley tech jobs. Nearly all of the women said they had experienced sex discrimination during their careers, and they shared a lot in common. For instance, 84 percent of them had been told they were too aggressive, and half said they had heard the accusation on multiple occasions. In addition, 66 percent of the women had felt excluded from key networking opportunities because of their gender, 90 percent had witnessed sexist behavior at conferences and company off-site meetings, and 60 percent had fended off unwanted sexual advances (in most cases from a superior). More than 85 percent of the women had been the target of demeaning comments from male colleagues.

Nearly 90 percent of the women surveyed had encountered clients and/or colleagues who directed questions to male peers instead of to them. One of these women is a top executive who shares an experience from her career. She was once at a meeting with three men: two of her colleagues and the founder of another company. Despite the fact that the woman's background and skills were the most relevant to the discussion, the founder made it clear that he preferred talking to the other two men. She says he "didn't make eye contact, and didn't really listen to the questions I asked before answering."[17]

Widespread sex discrimination in the tech industry has led to serious problems for some of the largest and most well-known companies. One example is Google, whose corporate headquarters is in Mountain View, California. In September 2017 three former female employees filed a class action lawsuit against Google.

Collectively, their employment spanned from 2005 through 2016, and all had experienced sex discrimination for most of the years they worked for the tech giant.

One of the three, a software engineer named Kelly Ellis, resigned after four years of what she describes as a sexist culture. The other two women had similar complaints, with all three decrying the lack of opportunities for advancement and being paid lower wages than their male colleagues. "It was time to stand up and say, 'This isn't OK, this isn't fair, and no more,'" says Ellis. "It really feels like a good time to be bringing this lawsuit, because people are waking up to the fact that sexism is pervasive and real in Silicon Valley and in the technology industry."[18]

> "People are waking up to the fact that sexism is pervasive and real in Silicon Valley and in the technology industry."[18]
>
> —Kelly Ellis, a former software engineer at Google

Pregnant women in the workforce can expect to be penalized for taking time off work once their child is born. Returning mothers tend to be paid less than men who are doing similar jobs.

Salary Inequalities

Google is one of numerous employers that have been chastised for salary-related sex discrimination, an issue that is more common than many people realize. According to a 2017 report by the Institute for Women's Policy Research, even though women make up nearly half the workforce, they earn considerably less than men. There is about a 20 percent pay gap between what men earn and what women earn—even when they are performing the exact same job. That has been the case for all the years women have been part of the workforce.

The fact that this male versus female pay gap exists has been well established—but *why* it exists cannot be easily explained. According to Olivia Mitchell, a director at the University of Pennsylvania's Wharton School, many different factors are involved. One of the most significant factors, says Mitchell, is women being "penalized" for taking time off to have children. Research has shown that working mothers are perceived as less valuable and less committed to their jobs compared with men and working women who do not have children. "Time out of the labor force is a penalty," says Mitchell. Two other factors that play a significant role in the pay gap between men and women are women's lack of negotiation skills (or inability to be forthright in asking for what they want) and the bias women face from their employers, meaning "not rating women as highly, and not paying them their due,"[19] Mitchell says.

Formidable Challenges

From the US military to Silicon Valley's tech companies, sex discrimination has been shown to be a serious, pervasive problem. It may involve biased hiring, a sexist work culture, different behavioral standards for males versus females, and/or unequal wages for the same job, just to name a few examples. Even though there are some promising signs of improvement, experts who study sex discrimination warn that there is a long way to go before males and females receive equal treatment in the workplace.

CHAPTER 2

Sexual Harassment

Sexual harassment has received an enormous amount of media attention in recent years. Highly publicized scandals involving famous celebrities have pushed sexual harassment into the limelight. As a result, public awareness of an issue that was long ignored, hushed up, trivialized, or dismissed altogether is now greater than ever before. A number of factors have contributed to the increased awareness, but one stands out from the rest: an October 5, 2017, *New York Times* article that exposed decades of sexual harassment and predatory behavior by film producer Harvey Weinstein. An in-depth investigation by *Times* reporters Jodi Kantor and Megan Twohey revealed serious allegations against Weinstein, most of which had never before been disclosed.

The reporters combed through documented interviews with current and former employees, legal records, e-mails, and other documents. The investigation revealed that for nearly thirty years, Weinstein had sexually harassed numerous actresses, assistants, and colleagues. In a 2015 memo to executives at one of Weinstein's businesses, former employee Lauren O'Connor wrote, "There is a toxic environment for women at this company." O'Connor, who was reportedly sexually harassed by Weinstein on multiple occasions, described how helpless his actions made her feel: "I am a 28 year old woman trying to make a living and a career. Harvey Weinstein is a 64 year old, world famous man and this is his company. The balance of power is me: 0, Harvey Weinstein: 10."[20]

A Matter of Power

With her "balance of power" remark, O'Connor was referring to one of the most fundamental aspects of sexual harassment: the offender having power over others. Studies have shown that those who sexually harass tend to be people with power and/or authority over other people, and they are most often male. "Sexual harassment is, above all, a manifestation of power relations," says the nonprofit organization Advocates for Human Rights. "Women are much more likely to be victims of sexual harassment precisely because they more often than men lack power, are in more vulnerable and insecure positions, lack self-confidence, or have been socialized to suffer in silence."[21]

> "Sexual harassment is, above all, a manifestation of power relations."[21]
>
> —Advocates for Human Rights, an advocacy group based in Minneapolis, Minnesota

When sexual harassment offenders are in positions of authority, such as management or supervisory roles, they have even more power. They often get away with nefarious behavior because the people they harass are too intimidated and/or afraid to speak out. Psychoanalyst Lyn Yonack explains, "They have what their victims, who are in less powerful positions, want and need: a job, good grades, a promotion, a recommendation, an audition, a role in a movie. . . . They confuse and control by dangling enticements with one hand and wielding threats, implied or explicit, with the other."[22]

This is a fitting description of Weinstein, who at the time of his downfall was an immensely powerful man. Along with his brother, he founded the mega entertainment company Miramax in Los Angeles, California, and another film group called the Weinstein Company. As one of Hollywood's top film producers, Weinstein won many prestigious awards, including six Best Picture Oscars. He was extremely wealthy, famous, and influential—and according to numerous women, he abused his power by being a serial sexual harasser. Young actresses, for instance, were sometimes told by Weinstein or one of his associates to report to a hotel ostensibly for work reasons. But once they arrived, they learned that he had very different ideas.

This scenario happened to Emily Nestor, who accepted a temporary job at the Weinstein Company when she was a law and business school student. On her first day Weinstein invited her to meet him for breakfast at the Peninsula Hotel in Beverly Hills, California. Thinking they would be discussing her new job, she accepted without hesitation. As they talked, though, she learned of his real intentions. Weinstein boasted about helping many famous

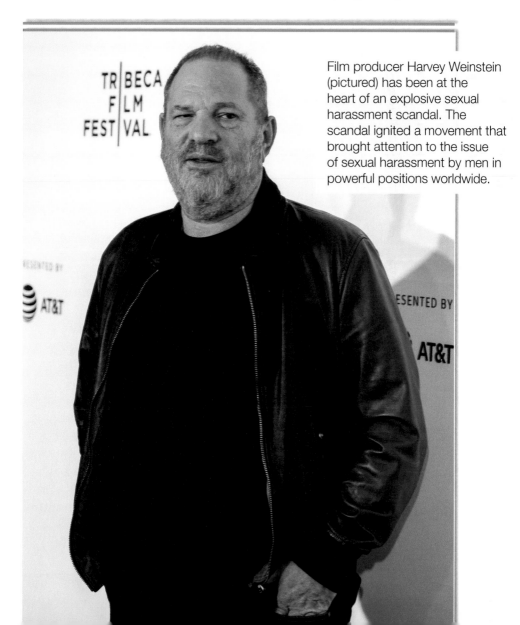

Film producer Harvey Weinstein (pictured) has been at the heart of an explosive sexual harassment scandal. The scandal ignited a movement that brought attention to the issue of sexual harassment by men in powerful positions worldwide.

actresses become successful, and he offered to do the same for Nestor if she had sexual relations with him. Although she refused over and over, he was very persistent with her. Finally, she left the hotel feeling frustrated and disillusioned that he showed no interest whatsoever in her professional qualifications.

Unwanted Behavior

Making inappropriate sexual advances is the best-known and often the most serious type of sexual harassment, but it is not the only type. Any unwelcome sexual behavior, whether demonstrated physically, verbally, or in writing, that makes an individual

A Famous Case of Sexual Harassment

Today there is increased public awareness that sexual harassment is a problem. But this was not the case in the 1980s, when the issue was rarely talked about. The turning point came in October 1991, when allegations by law professor Anita Hill against a judge named Clarence Thomas propelled sexual harassment into the national spotlight. Thomas had been nominated for the position of US Supreme Court justice. Hill had worked as Thomas's personal assistant years before. During Senate confirmation hearings, she testified about Thomas's lewd behavior toward her while he was her boss.

According to Hill, Thomas had repeatedly urged her to date him, even though she kept turning him down. "I thought that by saying 'no' and explaining my reasons, my employer would abandon his social suggestions," Hill said. "However, to my regret, in the following few weeks he continued to ask me out on several occasions. He pressed me to justify my reasons for saying 'no' to him." Also, Hill testified, Thomas subjected her to inappropriate discussions about sexual acts, body parts, and pornographic films. "These incidents took place in his office or mine," she said. "They were in the form of private conversations which would not have been overheard by anyone else." Thomas denied the allegations and was confirmed as a Supreme Court justice. But Hill's willingness to make her experience public helped bring the workplace sexual harassment issue out into the open.

Quoted in Library of Congress, "Nomination of Judge Clarence Thomas to Be Associate Justice of the Supreme Court of the United States," October 11–13, 1991. www.loc.gov.

feel intimidated or humiliated can be considered sexual harassment. This behavior includes inappropriate touching or leering at someone, making suggestive or obscene remarks, or making inappropriate implications in one's talk or actions. Some examples include sharing explicit photos or videos with coworkers, sending a suggestive e-mail to a colleague, telling dirty jokes, and making inappropriate remarks about someone's body.

Sexual harassment is not always blatant or obvious. Sometimes the words or actions are more subtle, as attorney Minna Kotkin explains: "You know, someone constantly commenting on how you look or what you're wearing or who your boyfriend is or where you're going on a date."[23] Subtle sexual harassment could include standing too close to a coworker or talking in a way that seems uncomfortably intimate. A man might lay his hand on a woman's knee when they are sitting together at a meeting or tell her that her dress nicely shows off her body. A female might try to persuade a man who works for her to get together at a bar outside of work. These and many other behaviors may not be obvious to everyone, but they can still be considered sexual harassment.

> "Harassment is illegal when it is so frequent or severe that it creates a hostile or offensive work environment."[24]
>
> —The EEOC, which enforces civil rights laws against workplace discrimination

It is often difficult, however, for sexual harassment to be proved, or even to distinguish whether certain behavior was actually harassment. Did someone intentionally touch a female coworker's breast, or was it merely an accidental brushing against her? Was a female manager's remark meant to be sexually suggestive, or was she just kidding around? Although a coworker's behavior may be annoying and even insulting on occasion, this does not necessarily constitute sexual harassment. The EEOC explains, "Although the law doesn't prohibit simple teasing, offhand comments, or isolated incidents that are not very serious, harassment is illegal when it is so frequent or severe that it creates a hostile or offensive work environment."[24] It is also illegal, according to the EEOC, when it results in individuals being demoted or fired from their jobs.

A Common Problem

The EEOC compiles sexual harassment complaints, and nearly sixty-seven hundred were reported during 2017. Yet the commission says that sexual harassment incidents are vastly underreported—an estimated three out of four individuals who experience sexual harassment never report it to a manager, supervisor, or union representative. The EEOC's Chai R. Feldblum and Victoria A. Lipnic write, "Employees who experience harassment fail to report the harassing behavior or to file a complaint because they fear disbelief of their claim, inaction on their claim, blame, or social or professional retaliation."[25]

Despite the underreporting of sexual harassment, publicity in recent years has led to many people opening up about their own experiences. Social media has played an important role in this openness, largely because of a movement known as #MeToo. Originally conceived by New York City activist Tarana Burke in 2006, the #MeToo movement went viral because of actress Alyssa Milano in October 2017. Upon hearing about Weinstein's years of predatory behavior against women, Milano was furious. It motivated her to find out how many others had experienced sexual harassment or assault.

On October 15, 2017, Milano sent out a tweet saying that she wanted to find out how widespread the sexual harassment problem was. She concluded with a request: "If you've been sexually harassed or assaulted, write 'me too' as a reply to this tweet." The next morning she discovered fifty-five thousand replies and the #MeToo hashtag trending at number one on Twitter. From then until mid-December, tens of millions of people in more than eighty-five countries have posted on Facebook or tweeted with the #MeToo hashtag. "It's really inspiring to think this might continue and things might change,"[26] says Milano.

The explosive growth of the #MeToo movement sparked another type of effort: better research collection on the prevalence of sexual harassment. This sort of information has long been collected for rape cases, but very little data has been compiled on sexual

Not all obnoxious behavior meets the legal definition of sexual harassment. However, federal officials urge employees who believe they are experiencing such behavior to report it to a supervisor or file a formal complaint.

harassment. In January 2018 a nonprofit group called Stop Street Harassment launched an online survey that involved approximately one thousand women and one thousand men aged eighteen and older. The survey found that sexual harassment and assault pose a significant problem, especially for women. More than 80 percent of females and 43 percent of males reported experiencing sexual harassment and/or assault at some point during their lives.

Of those respondents, 77 percent of women and 34 percent of men had experienced verbal sexual harassment; 51 percent of women and 17 percent of men had been touched in a sexual and unwanted way; and 41 percent of women and 22 percent of men had experienced cyber sexual harassment. "The findings show that this is a pervasive problem and permeates all sectors of our lives,"[27] says Holly Kearl, lead author of the study. She adds that most people who reported experiencing sexual harassment had experienced it in multiple locations.

Another finding of the survey was that victims of sexual harassment rarely confronted their harassers. Instead, they made

One Young Man's Story

Research has shown that women are sexually harassed far more than men. But it does happen to men, as one young man writes: "Rarely do we hear stories of men being sexually harassed by women at work, but that doesn't mean it doesn't happen." The reason he can say that is because of his own personal experience with a female coworker at his former place of employment. On one occasion, the woman remarked that she liked how he smelled. "Honestly," he says, "maybe she just liked the cologne I was wearing but if I said the same in the same situation would it be appropriate? Can I tell a woman, 'You smell good,' while we are working? If she reported that comment to human resources, would HR brush it off or would I find myself in trouble?"

In another instance, the woman laid her hand on his arm and asked if he had been working out. "Why was she touching me at all?" he asks. "I knew if I had been the one to touch her body I would be unemployed." He did not want the woman to get in trouble, so he decided to address the issue directly with her. He sent her an e-mail in which he described the incidents and asked that she keep their relationship professional. She apologized, and the inappropriate behavior stopped.

Quoted in Samara Lynn, "[Opinion]: This Male Millennial Wants You to Know: Women Harass Men Too," *Black Enterprise*, November 14, 2017. www.blackenterprise.com.

changes in their lives to avoid the harassers, such as modifying their usual routines or traveling different routes when they walked somewhere. Anita Raj, who directs the Center on Gender Equity and Health at the University of California–San Diego, says that this was the case with her teenage daughter. A few years ago the girl suddenly stopped walking to the public library by herself because she had been sexually harassed by a group of teenage boys. Raj says her daughter was walking in an affluent, safe area in the middle of the afternoon when the harassment happened. Because the boys were catcalling at her and making lewd remarks like "nice hips,"[28] she became so uncomfortable that she would not walk alone anymore.

Vulnerability of Low-Wage Workers

The 2018 survey and other research conducted in recent years have shown that people of all walks of life have experienced sexual harassment. But it appears to be especially prevalent among certain types of workers, such as those in low-wage jobs. The high incidence of sexual harassment, according to Washington, DC, attorney Sarah Fleisch Fink, is because there is such a vast difference in wages and power between female employees and the men who supervise them. "An imbalance of power in people in two different positions is a big part of sexual harassment occurring," says Fink, "and I think that there's probably nowhere that occurs more than in lower-wage jobs."[29]

The hospitality industry is well known for having a serious problem with sexual harassment. One survey that revealed the magnitude of the problem was conducted during the spring of 2016 by a union that represents hospitality workers in the Chicago, Illinois, area. Of the nearly five hundred women who took part in the survey, 58 percent of those employed by hotels reported unwanted behavior from guests, including flashing, groping, or being coerced into having sex. Of the casino workers and cocktail servers who took part in the survey, 77 percent said they were groped, pinched, grabbed, or in some other way touched without consent. Only about one-third of the workers said they complained to management. The majority of women felt that there was no point in doing so because their concerns would not be addressed.

Restaurant workers nationwide have opened up about experiences with sexual harassment, largely because the #MeToo movement has given them the courage to do so. According to the employee advocacy group Restaurant Opportunities Centers United, female waitstaff suffer from the highest rates of sexual harassment of employees in any other industry and endure all kinds of inappropriate behavior from customers. Twenty-five-year-old Lita Farquhar can attest to this problem. For the past decade she has been waitressing in New Orleans, Louisiana. She says that the old adage about the customer always being right is very much in place in the restaurant business. When servers are harassed and complain to managers, they risk being assigned the bad shifts or given less-desirable work. "It's really hard when a customer sexually harasses you," says Farquhar. "Because as a server, I make $2.13 an hour and I really rely on tips."[30]

Women who work in hotels and resorts are also frequently harassed while doing their jobs. Especially at risk are those who work in housekeeping, because they must work inside closed hotel rooms, away from video camera surveillance, and may be in rooms with male guests. According to research analyst Sarah Lyons, this situation exemplifies the importance of power in sexual harassment. "There is a very striking power imbalance between a woman who is cleaning a room and the man who often can spend hundreds of dollars a night on that room,"[31] says Lyons.

A member of hotel housekeeping staff changes bed sheets. Women who work in hotel and resort housekeeping jobs experience a higher risk of sexual harassment because they must work inside closed guest rooms.

A woman named Tina, who took part in the 2016 hospitality workers survey, has cleaned rooms at a downtown Chicago hotel for a number of years. Like many of her colleagues, more than once she has knocked on the door of a room and been greeted by a male guest who was naked. Because a coworker was physically attacked while cleaning a room, Tina worries that she could suffer the same fate. "I jump up every time I hear a door close, or if I hear someone talking in the hallway, I have to get up and look,"[32] she says. Also like her colleagues, Tina has been afraid to say anything, because if a guest complains about her, she could lose her job.

> "I jump up every time I hear a door close, or if I hear someone talking in the hallway, I have to get up and look."[32]
>
> —Tina, a housekeeping worker at a hotel in Chicago

The Plight of Military Women

Females in the military have experienced the same fears and frustrations as women in other types of employment. Research has shown that there is a serious problem with harassment among military women. Many have told of hostile work environments in which women are intentionally made to feel inferior to men. "At my first duty station at Camp Hovey in South Korea, my platoon sergeant told me very directly that all female soldiers were 'lazy sluts' and that I was going to become one too,"[33] says Supriya Venkatesan, who is a veteran of the US Army.

In November 2017 the Service Women's Action Network released a survey of more than thirteen hundred women from all branches of military service, including the US Coast Guard. The focus of the survey was to identify the factors that most affect the mental wellness of military women, including active duty and veterans. Overall, 60 percent of the women said that military

> "At my first duty station at Camp Hovey in South Korea, my platoon sergeant told me very directly that all female soldiers were 'lazy sluts' and that I was going to become one too."[33]
>
> —Supriya Venkatesan, a veteran of the US Army

service had a negative impact on their mental well-being. When asked what specifically about their military service most affected their mental health, 30 percent said it was sexual trauma, 11 percent cited sexual harassment, and 7 percent said gender bias and sex discrimination. Ellen Haring of the Service Women's Action Network found the survey results to be troubling. She says, "What is most distressing is that 49 percent attribute their poor mental wellness not to combat deployments but to the bias, harassment and sometimes assault that they received at the hands of fellow service members."[34]

Just the Tip of the Iceberg

Sexual harassment has been shown to be a problem nationwide in most every type of workplace, from a major film company in Hollywood to offices, hotels, restaurants, and the US military. Women are affected by sexual harassment far more often than men, but both men and women have reported experiencing it. Yet exactly how many people have been affected is unknown. Even though more people are speaking out, experts say there is no way to know, with any certainty, how serious and widespread the problem actually is. As campaigns like #MeToo continue to encourage people to speak out about their experiences, awareness of sexual harassment will undoubtedly increase, and perhaps its prevalence will begin to decline.

CHAPTER 3

How Do Laws Affect Sex Discrimination?

In March 2017 a judge in Tampa, Florida, ruled that Nestlé Waters North America, the world's largest bottled water company, had committed sex discrimination against a former employee. Attorneys from the EEOC filed the lawsuit on behalf of Dawn Bowers-Ferrara, who had worked for Nestlé's Tampa location as a finance and budgeting manager. In 2015 Nestlé created a new management position for which Bowers-Ferrara was highly qualified. She met all the requirements listed in the job description and had worked for the company for twenty years. She did not get the position, however. Nestlé instead selected a male employee who was less qualified than Bowers-Ferrara and then terminated her position. This termination was supposedly because of a consolidation of sales zones, but out of fourteen zone managers, she was the only one to lose her job—and the only zone manager who was female.

On September 21, 2015, attorneys from the EEOC filed a sex discrimination lawsuit on behalf of Bowers-Ferrara. About eighteen months later a judged ordered Nestlé to pay her $300,000 for back pay and compensatory damages. "The law of this nation does not allow for a woman who does her job well and gives almost two decades of her life to her employer to be held back by gender bias,"[35] says EEOC attorney Robert Weisberg. "The law of this nation" refers to federal legislation known as Title VII, which is one of numerous laws that exist to help protect people in the United States from sex discrimination.

Title VII

Title VII is part of a major antidiscrimination bill called the Civil Rights Act of 1964, which is divided into sections known as "titles." Each of these titles describes various types of places and situations where discrimination is illegal, such as public accommodations, public facilities, education, voting, and civil rights. The official name of Title VII, as stated in the Civil Rights Act, is "Equal Employment Opportunity." It prohibits discrimination in the workplace by specifying that discrimination is unlawful against employees or prospective employees based on race, color, religion, sex, or national origin.

Title VII generally applies to employers with fifteen or more employees, including federal, state, and local governments. The law also covers private and public colleges and universities, employment agencies, and labor organizations. Most every aspect of employment is subject to Title VII, including recruitment efforts, such as advertising, job fairs, and other ways of attracting potential employees. For example, according to the EEOC, "A help-wanted ad that seeks 'females' may discourage men"[36] from applying for a position and therefore violates the law. Also subject to Title VII are hiring practices; testing; wages; promotions; benefits, including retirement plans; use of company facilities; and procedures for discipline, discharge, and layoffs. Any employer who does not observe fair employment practices or who allows sex discrimination in the workplace is in violation of federal law.

An Unusual Beginning

In 1964, when the Civil Rights Act became law, it was only after months of debate in Congress. One issue of contentious debate was Title VII. As originally written, it banned employment discrimination due to race, color, religion, or national origin, and it contained no reference to sex discrimination. The National Woman's Party, a group fighting for equal rights for women, wanted that omission corrected. The group was aware of the legislation being

Job seekers talk to potential employers at a job fair. Title VII of the Civil Rights Act of 1964 prohibits workplace discrimination in all areas of employment from recruiting and job fairs to wages, promotions, and layoffs.

debated in Congress and saw it as an opportunity to afford women the same workplace protections that were being proposed for minorities. Also, says law professor and historian Robert C. Bird, "The amendment would provide all women job rights that were equal to men for the first time in history."[37]

Members of the National Woman's Party sought help from Representative Howard W. Smith, who was chair of the House Rules Committee. Smith was from Virginia and a known segregationist who was not in favor of civil rights legislation. He considered the women's request, however, because it gave him an idea. By making such a bold proposition during the congressional debates, it would inevitably create such a ruckus that the legislation might fail altogether. So he agreed to help the women in what Bird calls "a last ditch effort to sink the Civil Rights Bill."[38]

As Smith had suspected, when he announced his proposal to add the word *sex* to the Title VII section of the bill, the House erupted into pandemonium. Most members of Congress thought

Unequal and Unfair

Under federal law, an employee cannot be paid a higher or lower wage solely based on gender. The same is true of all other aspects of employment, including benefits. According to an August 2017 lawsuit by the EEOC, the law also applies to time off for child bonding after a baby is born. Whatever benefit is given to the new mom must also be available to the baby's dad.

The first-of-its-kind lawsuit was filed in 2015 by the EEOC against leading skin care and fragrance company Estée Lauder. The company's policy was for new mothers to receive six weeks of paid maternity leave after the birth of a child and six additional weeks for child bonding. New fathers were given two weeks for child bonding. When his child was born, Estée Lauder employee Christopher Sullivan challenged the policy and requested the same six weeks of bonding time that was given to the child's mother. The company denied Sullivan's request and offered him the usual two weeks for new fathers. He turned to the EEOC, which determined that Estée Lauder had violated Title VII, as well as the Equal Pay Act of 1963. "It is wonderful when employers provide paid parental leave and flexible work arrangements," says EEOC official Mindy Weinstein. "But federal law requires equal pay, including benefits, for equal work, and that applies to men as well as women." As of March 2018 the case had been settled, but no further details were available.

Quoted in US Equal Employment Opportunity Commission, "EEOC Sues Estée Lauder for Sex Discrimination," August 30, 2017. www.eeoc.gov.

he must be joking. They had seen him try repeatedly to block Title VII from becoming law, so this latest development was bewildering. When the noise quieted down, Smith assured his congressional colleagues that he was very serious about the amendment. "I do not think it can do any harm to this legislation; maybe it can do some good," he said. "I think it will do some good for the minority sex."[39]

As shocked and skeptical as House members were about Smith's radical idea, what came to be known as the "sex amendment" started gaining support. The few female representatives in Congress were strongly in favor of the amendment, and they let their colleagues know it. "These Congresswomen revitalized the debate and played a critical role in securing the amendment's ultimate passage,"[40] says Bird. Finally, the debates ended, and the sex amendment had gained enough votes to be formally written into Title VII. In mid-June 1964, both the House and Senate approved the Civil Rights Act and sent it to President Lyndon B. Johnson for his signature. He signed it into law on July 2, 1964.

President Lyndon B. Johnson signs the Civil Rights Act of 1964. The section of the law that prohibited workplace discrimination, Title VII, initially made no reference to sex discrimination.

Illegal Harassment

Even with the addition of the "sex amendment" to Title VII, nowhere in the law was there a reference to sexual harassment. In the 1960s, says historian Sascha Cohen, complaints about sexually predatory behavior in the workplace were "dismissed as trivial and harmless." Cohen says that women rarely talked openly about sexual harassment, but "the situation only became more pressing as their participation in the workforce increased throughout the 1960s and 1970s."[41] Then in 1986, with a ruling by the US Supreme Court, sexual harassment was declared illegal under Title VII of the Civil Rights Act of 1964.

The case was called *Meritor Savings Bank v. Vinson*. A bank employee named Mechelle Vinson said she was continuously

Where Sexual Harassment Is Legal

In the United States, Title VII of the Civil Rights Act of 1964 makes it illegal to discriminate against someone in the workplace based on sex. The law also includes sexual harassment. This legislation, by no means, has eliminated the problem, since people throughout the country have reported their own battles with sexual harassment. But in recent years, largely because of the #MeToo movement, numerous businesses, corporations, and other professional entities have vowed to do a better job of enforcing their policies in an effort to prevent sexual harassment. The movement has also helped people outside the United States; in fact, individuals from more than eighty-five countries have been inspired to open up about their experiences. But not all countries have laws that protect workers against sexual harassment.

According to a 2017 report from the WORLD Policy Analysis Center, sixty-eight countries have no workplace protections against sexual harassment. Most of these countries are in Asia, including the Arabian Peninsula, and some are located in Africa. Researchers Jody Heymann and Rachel Vogelstein write, "In many parts of the world . . . sexual harassment is not only pervasive—it is also perfectly legal."

Jody Heymann and Rachel Vogelstein, "Commentary: Sexual Harassment Legal Gaps in Many Countries," *Fortune*, November 17, 2017. http://fortune.com.

pressured by her supervisor to have sex with him, which she did on multiple occasions. If she refused his advances, which she reportedly often did, he became hostile and threatened to fire her. Finally, after taking extended sick leave from her job, Vinson was fired, and she filed a lawsuit against her supervisor and the bank. She lost her case in US District Court but later won on appeal. In March 1986, when the Supreme Court agreed to hear her case, it was the first time the high court had agreed to hear a case related to sexual harassment.

On June 19, 1986, the Supreme Court issued its unanimous ruling in Vinson's favor. Justice William Rehnquist delivered the opinion of the court, stating: "Unwelcome sexual advances that create an offensive or hostile working environment violate Title VII. Without question, when a supervisor sexually harasses a subordinate because of the subordinate's sex, that supervisor 'discriminate[s]' on the basis of sex."[42] Although this decision itself had little impact, historians consider it an important step in the fight against sex discrimination.

> "Unwelcome sexual advances that create an offensive or hostile working environment violate Title VII."[42]
>
> —William Rehnquist, a former chief justice of the US Supreme Court

In Pursuit of Equal Wages

Another important milestone in antidiscrimination laws occurred in June 1963 with President John F. Kennedy's signing of legislation called the Equal Pay Act. This law was the culmination of many years of effort to correct substantial wage differences between men and women in the workforce. Upon signing the Equal Pay Act, Kennedy pointed out that working women were only earning about 60 percent of what men earned. He referred to this as an "unconscionable practice of paying female employees less wages than male employees for the same job." Kennedy went on to acknowledge that the new legislation was only a beginning, but he considered it basic to America's democracy. He stated, "While much remains to be done to achieve full equality of opportunity . . . this legislation is a significant step forward."[43]

The Equal Pay Act states that men and women must be given equal pay for equal work in the same establishment. Their jobs do not have to be identical, but they must be what the law describes as "substantially equal." This means the jobs require essentially the same skills, effort, and responsibilities, and they are performed under similar working conditions in the same location. Career specialist and author Dawn Rosenberg McKay illustrates this with a scenario about two employees, Erica and Eric, who started new jobs at the same accounting firm on the same day. They both recently graduated from college, they have similar skills and experience, and their jobs are basically the same. They are headquartered at the same location, but both travel around the country to meet with clients. McKay writes, "The firm that employs Erica and Eric must pay them equal salaries because the work they are doing is considered, under the Equal Pay Act, 'substantially equal work.'"[44]

There are situations, however, in which unequal wages do not violate the Equal Pay Act and are justified. Continuing with McKay's scenario, if the two employees perform the same basic job but Eric has been at the company longer and has more seniority, he can be paid a higher salary. If Erica supervises other employees and Eric does not, their employer could legally pay her a higher wage. If they work in two different locations, and one lives in a city with a higher cost of living, a higher salary would be justified. McKay explains, "Their employer could pay Eric a higher wage if Erica works in Bismarck, North Dakota and Eric works in New York City."[45]

Slow Progress

Although the Equal Pay Act has been in force for more than five decades, male employees throughout the United States still earn more than their female counterparts. There has been improvement over the years, but statistics often vary widely. According to a 2017 report by the Institute for Women's Policy Research, for every dollar earned by a man working full-time, a woman working full-time earns 80.5 cents. The US Census Bureau estimates the figure to be 79 cents for every dollar paid to working men, whereas data from the Bureau of Labor Statistics show it to be 83 to 85 cents.

In recent years prominent companies have been sued for paying female employees less than males, including a number of Silicon Valley tech corporations. In January 2017, for instance, the US Department of Labor filed a lawsuit against Google. A lengthy investigation had revealed that the company was consistently and illegally paying women less than men. When the lawsuit was announced in April 2017, US Department of Labor official Janette Wipper stated, "We found systemic compensation disparities against women pretty much across the entire workforce."[46]

Many people wonder how companies can get away with such pay disparities between male and female workers. Although it is a complex issue, one answer lies in court rulings. In April 2017, for instance, a US Circuit Court of Appeals in Fresno, California, ruled that employers could legally pay women less than men if the difference is based on their previous salaries. Upon learning about the ruling, Stanford Law School professor Deborah Rhode denounced it, saying it was a step backward. "You can't allow prior discriminatory salary setting to justify future ones," says Rhode, "or you perpetuate the discrimination."[47]

Equality in Education

Although legislation has not ended wage inequality or stopped sex discrimination in the workplace, laws have reduced the prevalence of offenses. Another law that has made a positive difference is Title

IX of the Education Amendments. When this law went into effect in 1972, it became illegal for federally funded educational institutions, including schools, colleges, universities, and vocational programs, to discriminate against students on the basis of gender.

Many laws grow out of people's difficult personal experiences, and Title IX was no exception. One of its principal authors was Patsy Matsu Takemoto Mink, a Japanese American woman from Hawaii. Since childhood Mink's dream was to become a doctor, as she explains in a 1990 interview: "From the time I was four, I thought I was going to be a doctor, and some may have laughed, but nobody ever said, 'You can't be a doctor.'"[48] Later, however, that was exactly the message she received. After graduating from college in 1948, Mink began applying to medical schools—and one after another turned her down. After being rejected by more than a dozen, she abandoned her dream of becoming a doctor and attended law school. Several years later she opened her own law practice in Honolulu, Hawaii.

In November 1964 Mink became the first Asian American woman to be elected to the US Congress. Soon after being sworn in, she began working to get Title IX passed. It was a major challenge, since many of her congressional colleagues believed that it was wrong for the government to force schools to accept women. Mink and other supporters of the legislation fought hard, though, and they eventually won. On June 23, 1972, President Richard Nixon signed Title IX into law.

Although Title IX applies to all aspects of education, many people associate it exclusively with women's sports. This is because in addition to educational programs, the law also specified educational *activities*, meaning programs associated with schools such as athletics. As a result, Title IX has made a significant difference in athletic opportunities for girls and women. "Its most famous impact has been on school sports programs,"[49] says *Time* history and archives editor Lily Rothman. Since the law was passed, girls' and women's participation in sports and athletic programs has soared.

Representative Patsy Mink, a Democrat from Hawaii, was one of the principal authors of Title IX. The law, which took effect in 1972, made it illegal for federally funded educational institutions to discriminate against students on the basis of gender.

A Posthumous Victory

One of the most recent developments in sex discrimination legislation is a ruling on the case called *Zarda v. Altitude Express, Inc.* For many years, whether Title VII applies to sexual orientation has been a controversial issue. As of February 2018, with a ruling by a federal court of appeals on the *Zarda* case, people who are lesbian, gay, bisexual, or transgender (LGBT) are protected under Title VII.

The ruling stemmed from a 2010 sex discrimination lawsuit filed by Donald Zarda, a skydiving instructor from Long Island, New York. While preparing to take a female student on a tandem skydive, Zarda noticed that she seemed uncomfortable being strapped so tightly to him. So he told her not to worry because he was "100 percent gay."[50] When her boyfriend found out what Zarda had said, he complained to the school, and Zarda was fired. Zarda later filed a lawsuit against his former employer, claiming that his termination violated Title VII.

Two courts in New York initially ruled against Zarda. The US Department of Justice also got involved, stating its objection in a formal brief. But the February 2018 decision by the appeals court rejected those arguments and ruled in Zarda's favor. He was not able to savor the victory, however, because he was tragically killed in a 2014 skydiving accident. "I wish he could have been here," says Zarda's friend, William Moore. "He would have been so happy and elated that he changed this for LGBT people."[51]

Room for Improvement

From the passage of Title VII and the Equal Pay Act in the 1960s, to Title IX in the 1970s, the landmark Supreme Court case on sexual harassment in the 1980s, and the *Zarda* ruling in 2018, US legislators have made strides toward addressing sex discrimination. It has not been eliminated, however. Laws can help solve many problems, but sex discrimination is deeply ingrained in society and is a tough, highly complex problem to solve. Also, if people are unwilling to report sex discrimination—as most are—even the best laws can make little or no difference. Referring to sexual harassment legislation, the EEOC's Chai R. Feldblum and Victoria A. Lipnic write, "We have come a far way . . . but sadly and too often still have far to go."[52]

"We have come a far way . . . but sadly and too often still have far to go."[52]

—Chai R. Feldblum and Victoria A. Lipnic of the EEOC

CHAPTER 4

Challenges and Risks of Reporting Sex Discrimination

Of all the sex discrimination incidents that occur, only a fraction are ever reported. This is especially true of sexual harassment incidents. The EEOC received nearly sixty-seven hundred reports of sexual harassment in 2017 but estimates that three out of four individuals who are sexually harassed never tell anyone about it. They either go out of their way to avoid the harasser, deny or downplay the seriousness of the behavior, or try to forget about what happened, despite how emotionally painful that may be.

An Individual Choice

People choose not to report sexual harassment for a variety of personal reasons. For a young woman named Michelle, who was barraged with sexual comments by a senior co-worker, it was the fear that reporting him would be what she called a "lose-lose situation" for her. She explains why: "We get either accused of lying about it or we have to deal with repercussions—slut-shaming, being blamed for it. So there's really not much to gain by reporting it, other than your own personal sense of duty to yourself."[53] Surveys have shown that, like Michelle, most people who are sexually harassed believe that keeping it to themselves is the safest of all options.

One survey was conducted in November and December 2017 for the employment research firm CareerBuilder. More than eight hundred full-time adult employees across a variety of industries participated by answering questions about their experiences with sexual harassment. Of those, 17 percent of women and 7 percent of men said they had been sexually harassed at their workplace. More than half did not confront the person who harassed them, and even more chose to tell no one about it. When asked whether they had reported what happened, 72 percent said no, they had not.

Survey participants who opted not to report what happened were asked why they made that choice. For most, it was because they did not want to be labeled a troublemaker at their workplace. Other reasons given included the fear that they would be fired from their jobs and the challenge of trying to prove the offense. "It was their word against the other person's,"[54] says Ladan Nikravan Hayes, a career advisor at CareerBuilder.

Tough to Prove

Not being able to prove that sexual harassment actually happened is a common reason why so many people never report these incidents. Employment professionals and attorneys who specialize in sex discrimination cases emphasize that proving a harassment offense is notoriously difficult. It can even be challenging to pinpoint whether certain behaviors qualify as sexual harassment. Illegal offenses, according to the EEOC, include unwelcome sexual advances, inappropriate touching, requests for sexual favors, and other types of interactions (verbal and/or physical) of a sexual nature. This behavior must occur so frequently and be so severe that it creates a hostile and/or offensive work environment. But it is not always easy to draw the line between inappropriate sexual remarks and casual bantering and shop talk. Also, what one person finds hostile and offensive, another may consider playful and informal.

Along with these sorts of challenges, there is the matter of evidence, which is rare to nonexistent in sexual harassment cases.

Proving sexual harassment can be difficult partly because the behaviors that constitute harassment are not always clear. Illegal offenses include unwanted sexual advances and inappropriate touching—which might include repeatedly standing too close to another worker.

There are often no witnesses when one person sexually harasses another, as people tend to keep such behavior private and hidden. Attorney Debra Katz, who has specialized in discrimination cases for thirty years, explains, "When someone calls me, my first inquiry is, 'Who are the witnesses who can confirm this individual harassed you?'"[55] Even if coworkers do witness sexual harassment, says the EEOC, most say nothing because they do not want to get involved.

Christopher Partee did not remain silent about witnessing sexual harassment, and it cost him his job. Partee was a forklift operator at a warehouse in Memphis, Tennessee. He had a good working relationship with his supervisor; they were friendly and went to lunch together sometimes.

> "When someone calls me, my first inquiry is, 'Who are the witnesses who can confirm this individual harassed you?'"[55]
>
> —Debra Katz, an attorney who specializes in discrimination cases

Military Career Derailed

Most people who have been sexually harassed never report it out of fear that their employer will retaliate against them. This fear, unfortunately, is justified. Research has shown retaliation to be common in all kinds of employment, including the US military. There are numerous accounts of male and female military personnel who reported sexual harassment or sexual assault and ended up suffering for it. This is what happened to Emily Vorland, who joined the US Army after college and planned on a long military career as an officer. After two years of active duty, she was involuntarily discharged after reporting someone for sexual harassment.

At the time, Vorland was serving in Iraq. A higher-ranking officer propositioned her for sex, and she turned him down. She reported the incident to her commanding officer, who then relieved the man of his command. The man later appealed the decision, and the incident went to an investigative board. At that point, says Vorland, her character was attacked. The board determined that it was she who had acted inappropriately and threatened her with perjury charges if she refused to accept a general discharge for "unacceptable conduct." Believing she had no choice, she accepted the discharge with the plan to appeal it later. As of 2016 Vorland still hoped to get it changed to honorable but knew that was not likely. "I still feel pride in my service," she says. "But there's a sense of humiliation. I did the right thing, so how has this happened?"

Quoted in Mark Thompson, "Military Sexual Assault Victims Discharged After Filing Complaints," *Time*, May 18, 2016. http://time.com.

But nearly every day, Partee observed the man making lewd and sexually suggestive comments to the women who worked at the warehouse. So when one of the women approached Partee in tears and asked him to be a witness in a sexual harassment complaint, he agreed to speak to the supervisor—and was fired a few days later. Partee says he had a feeling something like that might happen, so he thought about not getting involved. "But if a woman is crying, I'm not just going to sit there and do nothing," he says. "I'm not going to walk away and not do something about it."[56]

Fear of Being Fired

The fear of losing one's job is a major reason why most people choose to stay uninvolved. Although it is illegal for an employer to retaliate against anyone who reports sex discrimination, retaliation is common—and so is being fired. *Washington Post* columnist Michelle Singletary explains:

> There are many factors that keep a woman quiet. But chief among them is money. They fear losing their ability to make a living. . . . It's easy to say, when you aren't faced with this type of situation, "I would tell." Or, "I would fight back." But what if fighting back meant a loss of income you desperately needed? What if it meant derailing a career in a field where it is already hard to succeed?[57]

There have been numerous documented cases of employees, most often women, who were fired for complaining about being discriminated against or being sexually harassed at work. When employers are faced with a lawsuit for illegal retaliation, many deny any wrongdoing and offer alternative reasons why an employee has been terminated. Often they blame the employee. This was the case with Tanja Vidovic, who was a firefighter with Tampa Fire Rescue in Tampa, Florida. Before being fired from her job, she had been the city's highest-ranking female firefighter.

> "There are many factors that keep a woman quiet. But chief among them is money. They fear losing their ability to make a living."[57]
>
> —*Washington Post* columnist Michelle Singletary

Hired in 2008, Vidovic was one of few females in the male-dominated fire department. From her first days on the job, she experienced sexual harassment, but she tried to overlook it. "There's a system in there when you're called like a rookie for the first five years," says Vidovic. "You're not supposed to talk. Harassment is supposed to be part of it. I was hoping it would end."[58] Rather than ending, however, the sexual harassment became more severe.

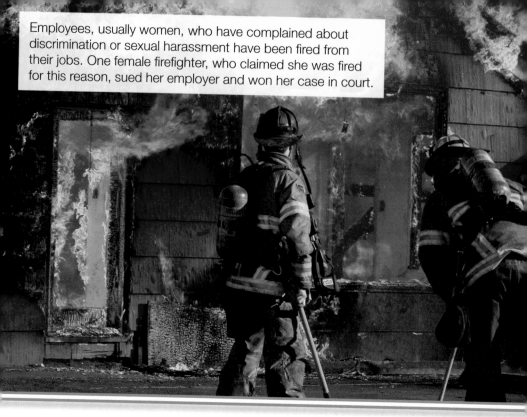

Employees, usually women, who have complained about discrimination or sexual harassment have been fired from their jobs. One female firefighter, who claimed she was fired for this reason, sued her employer and won her case in court.

Vidovic describes being peeped on by male colleagues while showering, having her breasts grabbed by a captain, and being sexually propositioned by another captain while they were out running together. She was the target of insulting, often obscene remarks by some of her male coworkers. When she asked for a female bathroom at the firehouse, she was mocked on a firefighter Facebook page. She was disciplined for petty infractions, while the same mistakes by her male colleagues were overlooked. Vidovic says she was also passed over repeatedly for promotions. After she became pregnant, she says a fire captain commented that "this would not have happened if she had kept her legs closed."[59]

On March 23, 2016, Vidovic filed a federal lawsuit against the city of Tampa, and the very next day she was fired. Fire department officials refuted her allegations about sexual harassment, claiming that she was terminated for untruthfulness. In December 2017, after a four-week trial, she won her case and was awarded $245,000 in damages by the City of Tampa. The following March, a judge ordered Tampa Fire Rescue to give Vidovic her job back.

Viewed as Troublemakers

Although Vidovic had the legal right to report the sexual harassment she endured, her reputation as a firefighter suffered because of it. This repercussion is an unfortunate reality for many people who speak out about what happens to them. Research has shown that those who report harassment incidents endure anger and hostility from company management, as well as lose opportunities for advancement. They develop reputations as people who are not team players or who have a bad attitude. "They become troublemakers—nobody wants to hire them or work with them anymore,"[60] says Jennifer Berdahl of the University of British Columbia Sauder School of Business.

This scenario is all too familiar for Lisa Kincaid, who has been a special agent with the Bureau of Alcohol, Tobacco, Firearms and Explosives (ATF) for more than thirty years. Over the course of her career, Kincaid has moved around to different ATF divisions and says she often saw signs of sexual harassment. "I used to think, it's just the way it is, and you have to go along to get along," says Kincaid. "Choose your battles."[61] Her perspective changed radically after she was assigned to investigate another female agent's harassment claims against a supervisor. That case, she learned, was just one of many, and what she discovered in her investigation was disturbing. Not only had a number of female agents been sexually harassed and bullied, some of them had been sexually assaulted.

After an extensive investigation, Kincaid turned in a 272-page report in August 2014 that spelled out the allegations of misconduct. She also continued to document additional findings afterward. Yet she says ATF senior management refused to open an investigation into the sexual harassment allegations or refer her findings to the review board that would have determined any necessary legal action. "In the end they didn't care about any of the women," says Kincaid. "I was told, 'They are not victims, they are complainants.'"[62] ATF management dismissed the seriousness of Kincaid's findings—and then demoted her to a lower-level position. She was passed over for promotions and other job opportunities, and her reputation at the ATF was damaged.

Challenges Faced by Freelancers

For many reasons, often the fear of retaliation, most people who are affected by sex discrimination never report it. If they choose to do so, however, they are protected under Title VII and have the legal right to report what happened to the EEOC—unless they work as freelancers. The way the law is written, in order to be covered by antidiscrimination laws, workers must be employed by an employer, rather than being independent contractors. That means more than one-third of the American workforce cannot take formal action against those who discriminate against them or sexually harass them.

This fact caused a serious dilemma for Amelia, a freelance writer from California. After receiving a sexually suggestive e-mail from a man who worked for one of her longtime clients, she was torn about what to do. She ended up forwarding the man's e-mail to the company's owners, who replied that they were "appalled" by what happened. The man was given a warning, and he left the company a short time later. But despite the owners' show of support, the client stopped sending her freelance work. Although retaliation against an employee who reports sex discrimination is illegal, it is another protection that does not apply to independent contractors. "When you're twiddling your thumbs waiting for work, all the 'what ifs' are rattling around in your brain," says Amelia. "In the back of my mind, I always wondered, am I not getting the work because I spoke up?"

Quoted in Leslie Albrecht, "Why Freelancers Face an Uphill Battle Against Sexual Harassers," MarketWatch, February 16, 2018. www.marketwatch.com.

As grossly unfair as it is, damage to one's reputation is a common by-product of reporting sexual harassment incidents. It happens often in jobs that have always been and still are male dominated and have what is colloquially termed "a bro culture." The ATF is one example; out of its 2,575 agents, only 356 are women. Another example is the US Forest Service, which employs thousands of people to fight forest fires. Out of more than 6,600 firefighters, 890 are female. The firefighting profession, according to union representative Jim Lopez, remains "one of the last strongholds in the Forest Service of male domination"[63] and, he adds, of male firefighters who are convinced that women do not belong in their profession.

One of the female firefighters with the US Forest Service is Abby Bolt, who is a battalion chief. Throughout her career she has faced bullying and harassment, but she typically kept quiet about it because she knew management would retaliate against her. In 2014, when she finally did file a sex discrimination complaint, the harassment intensified. She began receiving anonymous notes in her mailbox, such as one that warned, "You are a prime example of why women don't belong in fire, especially single mothers. Let it go."[64] She reported the notes but was brushed off by management, who said the investigation was closed because there was no one to be interviewed. Shortly after hearing that disheartening news, Bolt walked out to her vehicle and found the word *QUIT*, in huge letters, scrawled on the dusty back window. She was despondent over how she was being treated, but she refused to let anyone force her out of a job that she usually enjoyed.

Disbelief and Apathy

Because the risk of retaliation is so great, it takes a lot of courage for anyone who experiences sex discrimination to report it. So when the reaction an individual receives is unsupportive, it makes a bad situation even worse. According to Bryan Arce, a New York City lawyer who specializes in discrimination and sexual harassment, people often have a misconception about the role of human resources (HR). Rather than being advocates for employees, the department's first loyalty is to the company. "The HR department has an inherent interest in helping the company," says Arce, "because the company's name is on their paycheck."[65]

There are many cases in which employees have reported sex discrimination and have been totally brushed off by HR personnel. This was true of Susan Fowler, who reported sexual harassment at the

> "The HR department has an inherent interest in helping the company because the company's name is on their paycheck."[65]
>
> —Bryan Arce, a lawyer who specializes in discrimination and sexual harassment

ride-hailing company Uber Technologies. In November 2015 Fowler was hired as an engineer at Uber. Shortly after starting her new job, she began getting provocative chat messages from her manager, saying he was looking for someone to have sex with. Fowler was shocked, and she took screenshots of the messages to share with HR. But when she reported the man's actions, she says she was told that even though it was clearly sexual harassment, "it was this man's first offense, and that they wouldn't feel comfortable giving him anything other than a warning and a stern talking-to."[66] She was then given two choices: stay with the current team and risk getting a negative performance review or transfer to a new team.

Fowler transferred to a different team to get away from the man, and she started talking with other female engineers. She learned that they had had similar experiences with sexual harassment, including some who were propositioned by the same manager. Over the following months she continued to report what was happening, again with no support from HR or company management. Finally, after working at Uber for a year, Fowler quit her job and accepted a position at a different company. On February 19, 2017, she published an essay on her blog titled "Reflecting on One Very, Very Strange Year at Uber." It chronicled her time at Uber, how rampant sexual harassment was at the company, and how it was brushed off or ignored by company management and the HR department.

Fowler's essay, which was retweeted tens of thousands of times, gained national attention. Other women working in the tech industry felt comfortable opening up about their own stories of sexual harassment, as one woman commented on Fowler's blog: "Putting your story out there is incredibly risky, and you will probably get a lot of haters and headache for your effort. But, as a woman in tech: thank you so much for making your voice heard."[67] In June 2017, exactly four months after Fowler's essay appeared on her blog, Uber founder and chief executive officer Travis Kalanick announced his resignation.

Employees who report sex discrimination to their company's human resources department do not always get the response they expected. Some HR personnel try to help resolve problems, while others see their role as representing the company's interests.

Brighter Days Ahead?

It is a known fact that reporting any type of sex discrimination is risky. People's reputations have been ruined, they have been fired from their jobs, and in many cases they receive little or no support from company management or HR personnel. For these reasons and others, those who experience sex discrimination often keep quiet about it. But because of the actions of whistle-blowers like Fowler, along with increased public awareness of the problem, more people are finding the courage to speak up. "It used to be that women rarely were willing to go public with this," says Stanford Law School professor Deborah Rhode, "and I think we're now seeing a . . . change in that view."[68]

CHAPTER 5

What Can Be Done About Sex Discrimination?

Once an obscure, rarely discussed issue, sex discrimination is now widely known as a serious problem. As awareness has grown, companies big and small have been forced to recognize that the problem exists, it is not going to disappear on its own, and steps must be taken to combat it. One of these companies has a great deal of clout in Silicon Valley and seeks to be an industry leader in the fight against sex discrimination. That company is Facebook.

Beyond What the Law Requires

After spending an immense amount of time developing its new sexual harassment policy, Facebook rolled it out on December 8, 2017. In an unusual move, Facebook made the policy available to the public. Company officials hope that the policy can serve as a model for other companies that are struggling with how to address sex discrimination and harassment problems.

In a letter posted on the Facebook Newsroom, Facebook chief operating officer Sheryl Sandberg and Lori Goler, vice president of people, write:

Harassment, discrimination, and retaliation in the workplace are unacceptable but have been tolerated for far too long. These are complicated issues, and while we don't believe any company's enforcement or policies are perfect, we think that sharing best practices can help us all improve, especially smaller companies that may not have the resources to develop their own policies.[69]

Facebook officials wanted their employees, as well as people outside the company, to know they were serious about preventing sex discrimination, sexual or any other form of harassment, and bullying. So, Sandberg and Goler explain, the new policy goes "above and beyond what is required by law." Facebook's policy prohibits intimidating, offensive, and sexual conduct, even when such conduct does not necessarily meet the legal standard of harassment. "Even if it's legally acceptable," Sandberg and Goler write, "it's not the kind of behavior we want in our workplace."[70] The policy emphasizes that trying to excuse inappropriate behaviors by making remarks such as "I was just joking" or "I didn't mean it the way you took it" is not acceptable. Being under the influence of alcohol or other substances is also an unacceptable excuse for breaking the company's antidiscrimination policy.

Guiding Principles

At the heart of Facebook's new policy are underlying philosophies the company refers to as guiding principles. The first involves setting the standard for respectful behavior at work so employees know exactly what is expected of them. To facilitate this, Facebook developed harassment training for all employees and managers, as well as a program that focuses on unconscious bias. As the name implies, unconscious bias occurs unconsciously, meaning without someone being aware of it. It involves prejudicial thoughts and judgments that the brain forms quickly and automatically based on an individual's background, personal experiences, and societal stereotypes, among other factors.

Additional guiding principles include treating all claims and the people who voice them with seriousness, urgency, and respect; creating an investigative process that protects employees from stigma or retaliation; and taking swift, decisive action when an investigation

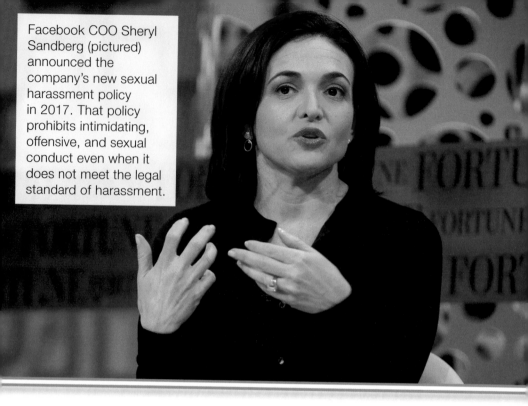

Facebook COO Sheryl Sandberg (pictured) announced the company's new sexual harassment policy in 2017. That policy prohibits intimidating, offensive, and sexual conduct even when it does not meet the legal standard of harassment.

determines that wrongdoing has occurred. "We have a zero tolerance policy," Sandberg and Goler state, "and that means that when we are able to determine that harassment has occurred, those responsible are fired."[71] If an investigation should prove inconclusive and it comes down to just one person's word against another's, Facebook management will take whatever actions are necessary to help everyone involved feel assured that they have been heard.

Another essential part of Facebook's new policy is the philosophy that everyone plays a role in keeping the workplace safe. Therefore, employees are encouraged and managers are required to report any violations of the policy, as well as suspected violations. Facebook officials want employees to understand that by remaining silent or looking the other way when they observe or suspect any form of discrimination or harassment, they share the guilt. Sandberg explains, "People need to be afraid not just of doing these things, but also of not doing anything when someone around them does it. If you know something is happening and you fail to take action, whether you are a man or a woman—especially when you are in power—you are responsible, too."[72]

People Helping People

Like Facebook, companies throughout the United States are becoming more aware of the prevalence of sex discrimination. Executives from these companies are also realizing that employees need to recognize the signs of sex discrimination and take an active role in helping quash it by speaking out. "It's really on all of us," says Kimberly Churches, who is chief executive officer of the American Association of University Women. "It's the responsibility of every employee. If you see something, say something."[73]

Holding people accountable for not speaking up about sex discrimination or sexual harassment is a crucial step in preventing these behaviors. Although most incidents of sexual harassment are not witnessed by anyone, when employees do witness such acts, they often remain silent out of fear that their employer will retaliate against them. A 2018 survey of 1,223 full-time workers by the Society for Human Resource Management showed this to be true. Among those who said they had witnessed sexual harassment in their workplace, only about one-quarter said they had reported it. The main reason given for opting not to report these incidents was the fear of retaliation.

> "If you know something is happening and you fail to take action, whether you are a man or a woman—especially when you are in power—you are responsible, too."[72]
>
> —Sheryl Sandberg, chief operating officer of Facebook

Often when people fail to report sexual harassment, it is at least partly because they know the offender. "One of the things that I find most astonishing about the recent revelations of sexual harassment is how many people supposedly knew the harasser was engaged in bad conduct and did nothing," says Leah Lively, a discrimination attorney from Portland, Oregon. "It's easier to look the other way than to report harassment—especially when the harasser is a person of power."[74]

Famed Hollywood film director Quentin Tarantino is an example of someone who ignored persistent sexual harassment when it was committed by a person he knew. In an October 2017 interview

"It's easier to look the other way than to report harassment— especially when the harasser is a person of power."[74]

—Leah Lively, a discrimination attorney from Portland, Oregon

with the New York Times, Tarantino admitted that he knew for decades about Harvey Weinstein's sexual harassment of women and said he now feels ashamed for not speaking up about it. "I knew enough to do more than I did," he says, citing several incidents involving prominent actresses. "There was more to it than just the normal rumors, the normal gossip. It wasn't secondhand. I knew he did a couple of these things." Tarantino says that even though he heard many alarming stories over the years, by doing nothing he failed to consider the full impact of what was happening to Weinstein's victims. He regrets that now. "I wish I had taken responsibility for what I heard,"[75] he says.

It is essential for people to start speaking up about sex discrimination and harassment, says Lively. She says this includes not only witnesses but also those who are personally affected by the behaviors. "It must be said that part of the responsibility for the current state of affairs is the failure of those who witness harassment and those who experience harassment to speak up, to report it, to challenge it, to expose it,"[76] she says. Lively adds that in some states such as Oregon, failing to speak up about sex discrimination could be considered aiding and abetting, which is a legal term used by law enforcement that stands for "helping and encouraging" someone who commits a crime. At the very least, says Lively, it should certainly be a violation of company policy. "Serious discipline of witness-employees who know of harassment and fail to report it should help eliminate it," says Lively. "By the same token, serious discipline must be levied against anyone who retaliates against an employee who has in good faith [reported] harassment."[77]

Changing the Culture

When people talk about how to combat sex discrimination, they invariably discuss the workplace culture—and how seemingly impossible it is to change it. "Sexual harassment requires a fun-

Anonymous Reporting

To help make their workplaces safer and free from sex discrimination, businesses, nonprofits, and government agencies have put new policies and procedures in place. Still, many people, fearing retaliation by their employer, hesitate to report what they see and choose to remain silent. A technology professional named Claire Schmidt is trying to change that with a new website she created called AllVoices. By using this website in their operations, employers are allowing their employees to report sex discrimination and related issues anonymously. The information can then be e-mailed to the person's manager or others in senior-level positions at the company so they can address the issue appropriately.

While creating the website, Schmidt spent months speaking with employees, employers, HR specialists, and others, and she heard the same thing over and over again: "People are afraid to speak up through fear of losing their jobs," says Schmidt, "and CEOs don't have access to the information they need to take necessary action." Schmidt was inspired to create the website by not only the need she saw in all kinds of industries but also her own personal experience with sexual harassment. "We are shaped by the experiences that we have," she says. "Sometimes really hard things happen which make us question 'Why me?' In my case, my experiences have made me want to fight harder for those who *don't* have a voice."

Quoted in Jennifer Savin, "A New Website Lets You Anonymously Report Sexual Harassment at Work," *Cosmopolitan*, November 15, 2017. www.cosmopolitan.com.

damental change in workplace culture, which simply does not happen overnight,"[78] says Jocelyn Frye, who is a senior fellow at the public policy research and advocacy organization Center for American Progress and a former deputy assistant to President Barack Obama. According to Frye, establishing new standards and expectations of appropriate conduct can seem threatening to employees and provoke resistance to change. But with a concerted effort by employers in all industries to combat sex discrimination problems, meaningful change can result.

One of the most important steps an employer can take, says Frye, is implementing antidiscrimination policies that are based on zero tolerance, which means a strict and uncompromising enforcement of the company's rules. It is essential for these policies to have the complete support of executive management. Frye explains, "Eliminating any form of harassment must begin with leadership from the very top of an organization."[79] As an example of a leader who mishandled a highly publicized sexual harassment case, Frye refers to President Donald Trump's unwavering defense of former Fox News personality Bill O'Reilly. By questioning the truthfulness of O'Reilly's accusers, says Frye, Trump was sending a message that women's complaints should be viewed with suspicion or not believed at all. "Whether it is the president of the United States or the manager at a local fast-food establishment, leadership is key to setting a harassment-free tone for the workplace,"[80] says Frye.

Another strategy that can help change workplace culture is for company management to establish equality as a core principle. According to Frye, doing so sends the message that everyone deserves equal treatment and an equal chance to succeed. "Sexual harassment undermines this core principle," she says, "by interfering with an individual's employment for reasons other than their ability to do a particular job." Equally important, says Frye, is work-

Fox news personality Bill O'Reilly (pictured with Donald Trump in 2015) was forced out of his job as a result of a series of allegations of sexual harassment and inappropriate behavior. Critics say Trump's defense of O'Reilly sends a message that women should not be believed.

ing collectively to combat bias (intentional or unintentional) and stereotypes. "It is critical to confront these barriers head-on," she says, "and not shy away from taking strong, deliberate steps to root out such perceptions and minimize their impact." These and other steps, along with a strong commitment to change the workplace culture, can go a long way toward ending sex discrimination. "Ridding the workplace of sexual harassment will take time—but it is possible," says Frye, "if we take action now."[81]

> "Whether it is the president of the United States or the manager at a local fast-food establishment, leadership is key to setting a harassment-free tone for the workplace."[80]
>
> —Jocelyn Frye, a senior fellow at the public policy research and advocacy organization Center for American Progress

Education and Training

In 2018, when Facebook released its new discrimination and harassment policy, the company explained its plan to develop training programs. These programs are designed to educate people about laws that prohibit sex discrimination and harassment, the types of workplace conduct that can be considered sexual harassment (along with examples), remedies available for victims, strategies to prevent sexual harassment, and numerous other components. Similar programs are being developed and put into practice by other companies that are also committed to reducing and eliminating sex discrimination. According to Jonathan Segal, an attorney who conducts sexual harassment training for supervisors, there has been a massive increase in training requests since the Harvey Weinstein story became public in October 2017. "I have often seen societal issues subject to intense workplace discussion, such as (the) 2016 election,'" says Segal. "I have never seen a workplace issue be the topic of this much workplace discussion."[82]

One company that has a renewed commitment to antidiscrimination training is Tempo Industries, an LED lighting firm headquartered in Irvine, California. Tempo has been conducting antiharassment training for its supervisors and managers every two years, including reviewing actions and words that can cause

The Ongoing Quest for Equality

Solving the serious, widespread problem of sex discrimination is a daunting task for which there are no simple solutions. Yet according to millions of women and women's advocates, a piece of legislation called the Equal Rights Amendment (ERA) would go a long way toward fixing the problem. The ERA makes discrimination on the basis of a person's sex unconstitutional, thereby prohibiting legal distinction between males and females in terms of property ownership, employment, and other factors. It was originally introduced in Congress in 1923, three years after the Nineteenth Amendment gave women the right to vote. Congress did not pass the ERA until 1972, but because enough states did not ratify it, it never became law. "Almost a century later, the ERA is still unfinished business," says ERA Coalition president Jessica Neuwirth. "That's right: Women still don't have constitutional equality."

According to Neuwirth, the ERA has been introduced in every session of Congress since it passed in 1972, but it has never made it to the floor for a formal vote. She says there is broad support for the amendment, which has been amplified since the growth of the #MeToo campaign. "Correcting our Constitution is long overdue," she says. "To truly create a new culture, one that promotes accountability for men and respect for women, we need to give women equal rights in the Constitution once and for all."

Jessica Neuwirth, "Unbelievably, Women Still Don't Have Equal Rights in the Constitution," *Los Angeles Times*, January 5, 2018. www.latimes.com.

a workplace to become hostile for employees. But Tempo's management decided to step up training efforts by using the sexual harassment cases dominating the media as "teachable moments." Martha Vaniman, Tempo's HR manager, explains, "It's a whole new world. You have all these different examples of what sexual harassment is in the media . . . it affects everybody, and we just need to make sure that we take accountability for not only acknowledging it but also being part of the solution."[83]

The Pentagon Cracks Down

Just as businesses and corporations nationwide have developed new sex discrimination policies, so has the US Department of

Defense. In February 2018 Pentagon officials formally announced the Harassment Prevention and Response in the Armed Forces policy. In doing so, they sent a strong message to service members across all branches of the military that sex discrimination in any form will not be tolerated. The new policy is very comprehensive and detailed, and it takes the place of old policies. It is designed to clarify and simplify the complaint-filing process for sex discrimination victims and assist them with getting help. It streamlines the procedure for making anonymous complaints—and, military officials emphasize, makes sure that those responsible for sex discrimination are held accountable for their actions.

Some of the listed offenses include offensive jokes, ridicule or mockery, insults or put-downs, displays of offensive objects or imagery, stereotyping, intimidating acts, threatening or provoking remarks, and veiled threats of violence. Prohibited sexual harassment was spelled out in detail in the policy, which refers to "unwanted sexual advances, requests for sexual favors, and deliberate

Some companies have instituted antiharassment training for supervisors and managers. Their goal is to prevent sexual harassment and discrimination in their workplaces.

or repeated offensive comments or gestures of a sexual nature to include forced or coerced submission, either online or in person."[84]

When the new policy was released, military officials emphasized that anyone who engages in such conduct will face a permanent blot on his or her service record. "Let me be clear: harassment has no place in our military," says Dana White, who is chief spokesperson for the US Department of Defense. "This policy brings us one step closer to eliminating these behaviors." According to White, the point of the military's development of the new harassment policy is to ensure that everyone has a safe workplace. "No one should be intimidated," she says. "No one should feel as though they can't do their job without being discriminated against, and this goes to hazing, this goes to political beliefs, this goes to religious beliefs." White adds that even though the military's new policy provides a formal binding foundation from which to work, it does not mean the military's work to end sex discrimination will be done. Rather, she says, "It's just the beginning."[85]

> "No one should be intimidated. No one should feel as though they can't do their job without being discriminated against."[85]
>
> —Dana White, chief spokesperson for the US Department of Defense

Optimism and Skepticism

Sex discrimination has been a problem for a very long time, but it is now receiving more attention than ever. No one, not even the most astute discrimination expert, knows the best way to solve the problem—or even whether it can be solved. But the renewed focus on sex discrimination by business leaders throughout the United States and officials from the US Department of Defense is a positive, promising step. New policies are being developed that are far more detailed and comprehensive than those of the past, and training programs for employees and managers are increasing awareness of what everyone can and must do to help achieve effective, lasting solutions to the sex discrimination problem.

SOURCE NOTES

Introduction: A Matter of Fairness and Respect

1. Quoted in Sam Levin, "She Took On Tesla for Discrimination. Now Others Are Speaking Up. 'It's Too Big to Deny,'" *Guardian* (Manchester), July 5, 2017. www.theguardian.com.
2. Quoted in Sheelah Kolhatkar, "The Tech Industry's Gender Discrimination Problem," *New Yorker*, November 20, 2017. www.newyorker.com.
3. Quoted in Olivia Solon, "The Lawyers Taking On Silicon Valley Sexism: 'It's Far Worse than People Know,'" *Guardian* (Manchester), September 2, 2017. www.theguardian.com.
4. Quoted in Levin, "She Took On Tesla for Discrimination.

Chapter 1: Sex Discrimination in the Workplace

5. Caryl Rivers and Rosalind C. Barnett, "8 Big Problems for Women in the Workplace," *Chicago Tribune*, May 18, 2016. www.chicagotribune.com.
6. Corinne A. Moss-Racusin et al., "Science Faculty's Subtle Gender Biases Favor Male Students," *PNAS*, October 2012. www.pnas.org.
7. Quoted in Bethany Brookshire, "Views on Bias Can Be Biased," *Scicurious* (blog), *Science News*, October 26, 2015. www.sciencenews.org.
8. Jennifer Lawrence, "Why Do I Make Less than My Male Co-Stars?," *Lenny Letter*, October 13, 2015. www.lennyletter.com.
9. Rivers and Barnett, "8 Big Problems for Women in the Workplace."
10. Quoted in Alexis Krivkovich et al., *Women in the Workplace 2017*, McKinsey & Company, October 2017. www.mckinsey.com.

11. Elizabeth M. Trobaugh, "Women, Regardless: Understanding Gender Bias in U.S. Military Integration," *JPME Today*, January 2018. http://ndupress.ndu.edu.

12. Roger Misso, "What It Means to Be an Ally to Women in the Military," *Task and Purpose*, December 27, 2017. https://taskandpurpose.com.

13. Quoted in Hope Hodge Seck, "Air Force Pays $140,000 to Settle Base Sex Discrimination Suit," Military.com, February 28, 2017. www.military.com.

14. Quoted in Seck, "Air Force Pays $140,000 to Settle Base Sex Discrimination Suit."

15. Liza Mundy, "Why Is Silicon Valley So Awful to Women?," *Atlantic*, April 2017. www.theatlantic.com.

16. Quoted in James Surowiecki, "Tracy Chou, 29: Bringing Tech's Dismal Diversity Numbers Out into the Open," *MIT Technology Review*, 2017. www.technologyreview.com.

17. Quoted in Emily Crockett, "A New Survey Explains One Big Reason There Are So Few Women in Technology," Vox, January 17, 2016. www.vox.com.

18. Quoted in Ethan Baron, "Google Hit with Lawsuit Alleging It Systematically Pays Women Less than Men," *San Jose (CA) Mercury News*, September 14, 2017. www.mercurynews.com.

19. Quoted in Madeline Farber, "Wage Gap: 3 Big Reasons It Still Exists on Equal Pay Day," *Fortune*, April 3, 2017. http://fortune.com.

Chapter 2: Sexual Harassment

20. Quoted in Jodi Kantor and Megan Twohey, "Harvey Weinstein Paid Off Sexual Harassment Accusers for Decades," *New York Times*, October 5, 2017. www.nytimes.com.

21. Minnesota Advocates for Human Rights, "Sexual Harassment," 2003. http://hrlibrary.umn.edu.

22. Lyn Yonack, "Sexual Assault Is About Power," *Psychoanalysis Unplugged* (blog), *Psychology Today*, November 14, 2017. www.psychologytoday.com.

23. Quoted in NPR, "We've Begun to Draw the Line, but It's Tough to Define Sexual Harassment," February 7, 2016. www.npr.org.

24. US Equal Employment Opportunity Commission, "Sex-Based Discrimination." www.eeoc.gov.

25. Chai R. Feldblum and Victoria A. Lipnic, "Select Task Force on the Study of Harassment in the Workplace," US Equal Employment Opportunity Commission, June 2016. www.eeoc.gov.

26. Quoted in Nadja Sayej, "Alyssa Milano on the #MeToo Movement: 'We're Not Going to Stand for It Anymore,'" *Guardian* (Manchester), 2018. www.theguardian.com.

27. Quoted in Rhitu Chatterjee, "A New Survey Finds 81 Percent of Women Have Experienced Sexual Harassment," NPR, February 21, 2018. www.npr.org.

28. Quoted in Chatterjee, "A New Survey Finds 81 Percent of Women Have Experienced Sexual Harassment."

29. Quoted in Alana Semuels, "Low-Wage Workers and Sexual Harassment," *Atlantic*, December 27, 2017. www.theatlantic .com.

30. Quoted in Yuki Noguchi, "Low-Wage Workers Say #MeToo Movement Is a Chance for Change," NPR, February 6, 2018. www.npr.org.

31. Quoted in Tanvi Misra, "What Some Cities Are Doing to Protect Hospitality Workers from Assault," CityLab, January 2, 2018. www.citylab.com.

32. Quoted in Misra, "What Some Cities Are Doing to Protect Hospitality Workers from Assault."

33. Supriya Venkatesan, "Military Women, Too, Should Serve Unmolested," *New York Times*, October 18, 2017. www.ny times.com.

34. Quoted in Service Women's Action Network, "Media Advisory: Service Women Identify Sexual Assault, Not Deployment, as Number One Factor That Negatively Affects Their Mental Wellness," November 10, 2017. www.servicewomen.org.

Chapter 3: How Do Laws Affect Sex Discrimination?

35. Quoted in US Equal Employment Opportunity Commission, "EEOC Sues Nestlé Waters North America for Sex Discrimination," press release, September 21, 2015. www.eeoc.gov.

36. US Equal Employment Opportunity Commission, "Prohibited Employment Policies/Practices." www.eeoc.gov.

37. Robert C. Bird, "More than a Congressional Joke: A Fresh Look at the Legislative History of Sex Discrimination of the 1964 Civil Rights Act," *William & Mary Journal of Women and the Law*, 1997. http://scholarship.law.wm.edu.

38. Bird, "More than a Congressional Joke."

39. Quoted in Bird, "More than a Congressional Joke."

40. Bird, "More than a Congressional Joke."

41. Sascha Cohen, "Before Anita Hill: History of Sexual Harassment in the U.S.," *Time*, April 11, 2016. http://time.com.
42. *Meritor Savings Bank v. Vinson*, 477 U.S. 57 (1986). https://supreme.justia.com.
43. John F. Kennedy, "Remarks upon Signing the Equal Pay Act," American Presidency Project. www.presidency.ucsb.edu.
44. Dawn Rosenberg McKay, "Equal Pay Act of 1963 Mandating Equal Pay for Men and Women," Balance Careers, February 13, 2018. www.thebalance.com.
45. McKay, "Equal Pay Act of 1963 Mandating Equal Pay for Men and Women."
46. Quoted in Sam Levin, "Google Accused of 'Extreme' Gender Pay Discrimination by US Labor Department," *Guardian* (Manchester), April 7, 2017. www.theguardian.com.
47. Quoted in Maggie Mallon, "How Employers Can Legally Pay Women Less than Men," *Glamour*, May 31, 2017. www.glamour.com.
48. Quoted in Tania Cruz and Eric K. Yamamoto, "A Tribute to Patsy Takemoto Mink," ASIAN-*Pacific Law & Policy Journal*, Summer 2003, p. 575.
49. Lily Rothman, "How Title IX First Changed the World of Women's Sports," *Time*, June 23, 2017. http://time.com.
50. Quoted in Alan Feuer and Benjamin Weiser, "Civil Rights Act Protects Gay Workers, Appeals Court Rules," *New York Times*, February 26, 2018. www.nytimes.com.
51. Quoted in Vanessa Chesnut, "Plaintiff at Center of Landmark Gay-Rights Case Never Got to Witness His Victory," NBC News, March 3, 2018. www.nbcnews.com.
52. Feldblum and Lipnic, "Select Task Force on the Study of Harassment in the Workplace."

Chapter 4: Challenges and Risks of Reporting Sex Discrimination

53. Quoted in Elizabeth Chuck, "Weinstein Lesson: Lot to Lose, Little to Gain by Reporting Sex Harassment," NBC News, October 13, 2017. www.nbcnews.com.
54. Quoted in Nancy Marshall-Genzer, "Why Most Employees Still Won't Report Sexual Harassment," *Fresh Air*, NPR, January 19, 2018. http://nprillinois.org.
55. Quoted in Alexandra Olson, "For Witnesses, Calling Out Sexual Harassment Is Complicated," *Chicago Tribune*, December 17, 2017. www.chicagotribune.com.

56. Quoted in Olson, "For Witnesses, Calling Out Sexual Harassment Is Complicated."

57. Michelle Singletary, "Why Don't Women Talk About Harassment? They Are Afraid to Lose Their Jobs," *Washington Post*, November 30, 2017. www.washingtonpost.com.

58. Quoted in Mitch Perry, "Bob Buckhorn Now Says Tampa May Not Appeal Firefighter's Sexual Discrimination Ruling," Florida Politics, February 22, 2018. http://floridapolitics.com.

59. Quoted in Dan Sullivan, "Tampa Fire Chief Testifies in Deposition for Discrimination Suit Against Department," *Tampa Bay Times*, January 6, 2017. www.tampabay.com.

60. Quoted in Claire Cain Miller, "It's Not Just Fox: Why Women Don't Report Sexual Harassment," *New York Times*, April 10, 2017. www.nytimes.com.

61. Quoted in Jessica Schneider, "ATF Agent Alleges Retaliation for Exposing Sexual Harassment at Justice Department," CNN, January 23, 2018. www.cnn.com.

62. Quoted in Shelley Murphy, "ATF Agent's Case Highlights Treatment of Women Within the Agency," *Boston Globe*, February 7, 2018. www.bostonglobe.com.

63. Quoted in Elizabeth Flock and Joshua Barajas, "They Reported Sexual Harassment. Then the Retaliation Began," *PBS NewsHour*, March 1, 2018. www.pbs.org.

64. Quoted in Flock and Barajas, "They Reported Sexual Harassment."

65. Quoted in Marie Solis, "How Human Resources Is Failing Women Victims of Workplace Sexual Harassment," *Newsweek*, October 19, 2017. www.newsweek.com.

66. Susan Fowler, "Reflecting on One Very, Very Strange Year at Uber," *Susan Fowler* (blog), February 19, 2017. www.susanjfowler.com.

67. Quoted in Hannah Jane Parkinson, "Good Riddance Travis Kalanick: One Woman's Victory Against Sexist Tech," *Guardian* (Manchester), June 22, 2017. www.theguardian.com.

68. Quoted in Jeremy Hobson, "How Laws Against Sexual Harassment and Abuse Work," *Here & Now*, WBUR, November 2, 2017. www.wbur.org.

Chapter 5: What Can Be Done About Sex Discrimination?

69. Sheryl Sandberg and Lori Goler, "Sharing Facebook's Policy on Sexual Harassment," Facebook Newsroom, December 8, 2017. https://newsroom.fb.com.

70. Sandberg and Goler, "Sharing Facebook's Policy on Sexual Harassment."

71. Sandberg and Goler, "Sharing Facebook's Policy on Sexual Harassment."

72. Quoted in Nicholas Kristof, "Steinem, Sandberg, and Judd on How to End Sex Harassment," *New York Times*, October 25, 2017. www.nytimes.com.

73. Quoted in Courtney Connley, "5 Ways Men Can Address—and Help Prevent—Sexual Harassment at Work," CNBC Make It, October 26, 2017. www.cnbc.com.

74. Leah Lively, "Sexual Harassment 2018: It Is Your Business," Davis, Wright, Tremaine LLP, December 12, 2017. www.dwt.com.

75. Quoted in Jodi Kantor, "Tarantino on Weinstein: 'I Knew Enough to Do More than I Did,'" *New York Times*, October 19, 2017. www.nytimes.com.

76. Lively, "Sexual Harassment 2018."

77. Lively, "Sexual Harassment 2018."

78. Jocelyn Frye, "How to Combat Sexual Harassment in the Workplace," Center for American Progress, October 19, 2017. www.americanprogress.org.

79. Frye, "How to Combat Sexual Harassment in the Workplace."

80. Frye, "How to Combat Sexual Harassment in the Workplace."

81. Frye, "How to Combat Sexual Harassment in the Workplace."

82. Quoted in Charisse Jones, "Sexual Harassment Accusations Changing Office Policies, Increasing Training at Work," *USA Today*, December 12, 2017. www.usatoday.com.

83. Quoted in Jones, "Sexual Harassment Accusations Changing Office Policies, Increasing Training at Work."

84. Quoted in Oriana Pawlyk, "Pentagon Unveils Policy to Combat Misconduct, Harassment in the Ranks," Military.com, February 8, 2017. www.military.com.

85. Quoted in Jeff Daniels, "Pentagon Takes On Bullying, 'Offensive Jokes' in New Harassment Policy," CNBC, February 8, 2018. www.cnbc.com.

ORGANIZATIONS AND WEBSITES

American Association of University Women

1310 L St. NW, Suite 1000
Washington, DC 20005
website: www.aauw.org

The American Association of University Women seeks to advance equity for women and girls through advocacy, education, philanthropy, and research. Its website offers information about discrimination-related issues, news articles, explanations of laws, and a search engine that produces numerous articles about sex discrimination.

American Civil Liberties Union (ACLU)

125 Broad St., 18th Floor
New York, NY 10004
website: www.aclu.org

The ACLU works with courts, legislatures, and communities to defend and preserve the rights and liberties that are guaranteed for all Americans under the US Constitution. Its website focuses on issues and rights and provides links to a number of publications about sex discrimination.

Equal Rights Advocates

1170 Market St., Suite 700
San Francisco, CA 94102
website: www.equalrights.org

Equal Rights Advocates exists to protect and expand economic and educational access and opportunities for women and girls. Its website offers a wide variety of publications such as *Ending Harassment Now*, which is for high school students; articles about sex discrimination and what is being done to stop it; and information on many more topics related to sex discrimination issues.

National Women's Law Center

11 Dupont Cir. NW #800
Washington, DC 20036
website: www.nwlc.org

The National Women's Law Center seeks to protect and promote equality and opportunity for women and families. Its website offers news releases, information about current issues, a state-by-state guide to antidiscrimination laws, and a search engine that produces fact sheets, legal documents, and a wealth of information about sex discrimination.

Service Women's Action Network

1015 Fifteenth St. NW, Suite 600
Washington, DC 20005
website: www.servicewomen.org

The Service Women's Action Network advocates for the individual and collective needs of women in all branches of the military. Its website features news articles, fact sheets, and other pertinent publications, including those related to sex discrimination and harassment.

US Equal Employment Opportunity Commission (EEOC)

131 M St. NE
Washington, DC 20507
website: www.eeoc.gov

The EEOC is charged with enforcing federal antidiscrimination laws related to any aspect of employment. The collection of materials available through its website is comprehensive, with the search engine producing a wealth of information on sex discrimination and related issues.

FOR FURTHER RESEARCH

Books

Karen Blumenthal, *Let Me Play: The Story of Title IX: The Law That Changed the Future of Girls in America*. New York: Simon and Schuster, 2005.

Gretchen Carlson, *Be Fierce: Stop Harassment and Take Your Power Back*. New York: Center Street, 2017.

Kerry Lester, *No, My Place*: *Reflections on Sexual Harassment in Illinois Government and Politics*. Cavehill, 2018.

Ellen Pao, *Reset: My Fight for Inclusion and Lasting Change*. New York: Spiegel and Grau, 2017.

Internet Sources

Natasha Josefowitz, "Why Do We Experience Gender Discrimination in Today's World?," *Huffington Post*, October 23, 2017. www.huffingtonpost.com/entry/why-do-we-still-experience -gender-discrimination-in_us_59ee6fe3e4b0f777352c8747.

Sheelah Kolhatkar, "The Tech Industry's Gender Discrimination Problem," *New Yorker*, November 20, 2017. www .newyorker.com/magazine/2017/11/20/the-tech-industrys -gender-discrimination-problem.

Jessica Lander, "Tackling Teen Sexual Harassment," *Boston Globe*, January 2, 2017. www.bostonglobe.com/opinion /2017/01/02/tackling-teen-sexual-harassment/XueH8daT m6t8kbTqg15b4I/story.html.

Kim Parker and Cary Funk, "Gender Discrimination Comes in Many Forms for Today's Working Women," *Fact Tank* (blog), Pew Research Center, December 14, 2017. www.pew research.org/fact-tank/2017/12/14/gender-discrimination -comes-in-many-forms-for-todays-working-women.

Sue Scheff, "Teens, Cyberbullying, Sexual Harassment, and Social Media: The New Normal?," *Huffington Post*, February 25, 2016. www.huffingtonpost.com/sue-scheff/teens-sexual-harassment-a_b_9310060.html.

Gillian B. White, "Beyond Sexual Harassment," *Atlantic*, December 14, 2017. www.theatlantic.com/business/archive/2017/12/women-work-discrimination/548432.

INDEX

Note: Boldface page numbers indicate illustrations.

PICTURE CREDITS